Different Tools *for* Different Learners

Language Arts Activities to Start Using Today

by Donna VanderWeide, M.S.

Crystal Springs
BOOKS

A division of SDE Staff Development for Educators (SDE)
Peterborough, New Hampshire

Published by Crystal Springs Books
A division of Staff Development for Educators (SDE)
75 Jaffrey Road, PO Box 500
Peterborough, NH 03458
1-800-321-0401
www.crystalsprings.com
www.sde.com

Published 2004
Printed in the United States of America
08   4 5

ISBN: 1-884548-66-0

Library of Congress Cataloging-in-Publication Data

VanderWeide, Donna, 1938-
   Different tools for different learners : language arts activities to start using
     today / by Donna VanderWeide, M.S.
    p. cm.
   ISBN 1-884548-66-0
   1. Language arts. 2. Individualized instruction. 3. Activity programs in
    education. I. Title.
   LB1575.8.V36 2004
   372.6—dc22   2004009141

Art Director, Designer, and Production Coordinator: Jill Shaffer
Illustrator: Bruce Hammond

If you become a teacher, by your students you'll be taught.

I dedicate this book to all the children I have taught over the years. To everyone from that very first class of special needs children who taught me how to reach the very "special" learners to those exceptionally gifted children who challenged me to state the "why" before the "how"—I want to say, "Thank you!" After 25 years of teaching the full spectrum of learners, I am still learning the "how" of teaching.

Contents

Acknowledgments

SPECIAL THANKS TO:

Vicki Alger, my special desktop writer, without whom this book would never have been written! Not only is Vicki a whiz with the computer and with helping me express my thoughts, but she is also the mother of three of my "gifted" grandchildren.

Sharon Smith, our dedicated Crystal Springs editor, whose wonderfully light sense of humor and well-placed questions and phrases have created a book for veteran teachers as well as for beginners.

Lorraine Walker, the publishing director at Crystal Springs, for her belief that this book needed a wider audience than that of my self-published edition!

Presenters and teachers I have learned from over the years, without whom I never would have been inspired to create half of these ideas for children in my classroom. We teachers borrow only from the best, so if you see a germ of your ideas in this book—thank you for sharing!!

Introduction

Teachers today are faced with a diverse student population that requires a different approach to instruction. No longer can we rely on rote memorization or on the set "scope and sequence" charts of the old basal system.

The multiple intelligence design of Howard Gardner *(Multiple Intelligences)* and the brain research strategies of Eric Jensen *(Teaching with the Brain in Mind)* have shown teachers that there is a better and more effective way to teach and reach *all* of the learners in our classrooms. That better way is differentiated instruction.

Different children learn in different ways. Each brings into the classroom his unique outside world of social, cultural, and intellectual curiosities. Each brings different intelligences and different skill sets. The challenge for the teacher is to find a way to meet government-mandated educational standards and at the same time address the learning styles and innate abilities of each student. In differentiated instruction, teachers and students work together to help students master the basic concepts and understandings necessary for success at each grade level.

Carol Ann Tomlinson, in her book *Differentiated Instruction,* gives several examples of classroom designs. Each of Tomlinson's recommendations can help in creating the differentiated approach that Gardner and Jensen recommend to meet the instructional needs of our students.

But with all these theoretical discussions, the question remains: "How do I do it in my classroom?" Or, put another way: "I've read all the theories. But how do I do it on Monday?"

Different Tools for Different Learners is a collection of practical, classroom-tested options for teachers to choose from as they make instructional decisions about their students. The possibilities for implementing differentiated instruction in your classroom are endless.

Just like the tools in your toolbox at home, the learning tools presented here are designed to meet multiple needs and serve multiple purposes—in this case, providing you with options to engage and motivate *all* your young learners. As you page through this book, you'll find games and activities that emphasize reading and writing and that get your kids moving and working together. You'll find Choice Cards to address different learning styles. You'll find task cards to keep students focused. You'll find assessment rubrics to help you evaluate student progress. And that's just a small sampling.

With all the varied tools included here, however, you'll also find certain recurring themes that are central to the concept of differentiated instruction. These include:

◆ **Collaboration.** Students need to build community and to feel that their classroom is risk-free. Teachers need to provide opportunities for students to exchange and support ideas. For the student who needs to move around and talk with others, collaboration exercises provide time to activate prior knowledge, think creatively, and cement new learning into long-term memory. Collaboration exercises also provide opportunities for teachers to observe and evaluate students as part of ongoing assessment.

◆ **Modeling.** Teachers need to take time to show students what "good, proficient" readers do as they negotiate different types of texts for different purposes or respond in writing to different genres. Modeling options will vary according to the age and maturity of the students. *Different Tools for Different Learners* gives you ideas on how to engage *all* students in instructional dialogue with the teacher and with each other.

◆ **Guided practice.** Feedback is critical in learning. A student needs to know the answer to, "Am I doing it right?" Children can give each other feedback while working in pairs and small groups. And this is also another opportunity for teachers to assess whether students are on the right track or more modeling is necessary.

◆ **Independent practice.** Students need to practice until skills are "perfectly permanent." But that doesn't mean that everyone has to practice in the same way, or even that each child must perform the same task over and over. Rather, you'll find options to suit all different learning styles and intelligences. Of course, the wide range of products that come out of independent practice will again help you to evaluate the quality and extent of student learning.

So here you have it: tools for multiple learning styles, intelligences, skill levels, and interests. You know the standards your state has established for you and your students. You know the needs of your class better than anyone. As a teacher, you're the ultimate decision maker and the ultimate craftsperson, teaching skills to a wide variety of young apprentices. The choices in the following pages will provide the tools they need for this huge job.

I'm confident that as you use these tools with your students, they won't just memorize the material. They'll learn how to learn. And you can't ask for anything better than that.

Comparing Classrooms

Which column describes your classroom?

TRADITIONAL	DIFFERENTIATED
The "Teacher Guide" determines where students start and what they study.	Teachers start instruction by focusing on student interests, skills, and abilities.
Students are measured against a preset standard of performance.	Each student's progress is measured in terms of his personal growth, indicated by the skills he masters and the knowledge he gains.
Students needing an accelerated curriculum are given more work at the same level. Students needing support are given less work.	Students are met with an appropriate rate of challenge based on their abilities and interests.
Measures of progress follow instruction.	Assessment goes on throughout the day and in several ways.
Whole-group instruction is the most frequently used method of transmitting information. Teacher talk dominates the classroom.	The teacher maintains a balance between modeling lessons for the whole group and engaging in dialogue and other interactions with individual students and small groups.
Commercially prepared drill sheets are the primary method of practicing skills.	Students use multiple methods of skill practice.
Students use a single text.	Children use many sources of print and picture support in the course of study.
Convergent questioning dominates; single correct answers are rewarded.	Questions are asked frequently by students as well as teachers. Open-ended questions spark divergent thinking and lead to additional questions and inquiries.
Instruction time is predetermined and relatively fixed for assigned tasks.	Students' needs and interests determine how much time is spent on a task or project.
Teachers or administrators set the standard of excellence for attainment of skills or standards of work.	Students and teachers work together to set the different levels of performance and determine the grade given for each level. Standards form the backbone of instruction, but the procedures to attain the standards and the subsequent evaluation options vary with the child.
Goals are predetermined by outside sources.	Individual growth from each student's personal starting point determines that student's personal goal of excellence.

The Multiple Intelligence Approach to Instruction

Children come to school with many different kinds of abilities. As teachers, we try to match up these abilities with our instructional approaches. That's the reason that each of the activities in the following pages includes notes on the specific intelligences addressed. These notes are designed to help you identify just the right activities for all the different learners in your class. These may include …

The construction learner: This child thinks in images and pictures. He loves drawing and designing three-dimensional models.

The nature learner: This child likes being outside. He usually has collections of shells, rocks, and bird nests, and has a keen interest in science.

The number learner: This child is interested in logical thinking. He enjoys math and puzzles, and likes to work with graphic organizers.

The on-my-own learner: This child prefers to work on his own. He enjoys independent projects and likes to set his own goals.

The on-the-move learner: This child enjoys touching things and moving through space. He is well coordinated and learns best when physically involved in activities.

The rhythmic learner: This child is attuned to music, rhymes, and rhythms. He responds to tones and beats in poetry, raps, and intonations.

The with-friends learner: This child seeks out other people. He works best with other students and is often a leader in the class.

The word learner: This child thinks in words. He expresses himself well and enjoys reading and writing.

In addition to these native abilities we call intelligences, each of our students has a preferred way of learning. Each activity in this book is designed with one or more of these learning styles (noted at the beginning of the activity) in mind …

Auditory: Some students assimilate information best by listening. Note, however, that auditory processing doesn't usually become a learning preference until fourth or fifth grade.

Tactile/kinesthetic: These children—especially those who are among our youngest students—must manipulate things in their environment. A tactile-kinesthetic child benefits from touching with her fingers and tongue (tasting and eating).

Visual: These students do best when given pictures combined with words (oral and/or written).

Of course, the idea here isn't to concentrate on just one learning style, but rather to include as many different styles as possible. Some children fall into more than one of these descriptions or exhibit different styles when engaged in different activities. As a general rule, the more avenues of input you can provide (auditory, visual, tactile/kinesthetic), the higher the possibility that each student will get the information he needs.

Activities

MODELING MINI-LESSONS
Overview

Y ou can improve your students' reading comprehension by modeling for them what a good reader thinks as she reads.

To introduce to your students the concepts that follow, you'll need to share with them text that's large enough so that they can see what you're reading as well as hear your explanations. This enlarged text can be a big book, a selected section of a chart, or an overhead of the chosen text. It doesn't particularly matter what the text is; it matters that they can see it and can understand how you're interacting with it.

Begin reading the text with the students—but pause frequently to share with the class your reactions to what you're reading. Try to include in your think-alouds these seven habits of good readers ...

Questioning: "What's going on right here?"

Inferring: "I think this character might be afraid, because before he said ..."

Predicting: "I bet this time he will ..."

Connecting: "This reminds me of another book we've read."

Imaging: "Wow! When I read that part, I got this great picture in my head about how the troll would look!"

Judging importance: "I think the one big idea from this book is ..."

Using fix-up strategies: "I'm confused about what that word means. I'm going to go back and read that sentence again."

The Teacher Task Cards in the following pages will help you to model "think-aloud" reading for your students. Once they understand the process, move on to the Student Task Cards. These cards, designed to be used by student pairs, offer a great way to build reading comprehension.

Teacher Task Cards for Think-Alouds

PURPOSE
To model good reading habits and improve student comprehension

INTELLIGENCE
Word learner

LEARNING STYLES
Auditory learner
Visual learner

GROUP SIZE
Small group (4–6)
Whole class

SKILLS
Evaluating
Fix-up strategies
Following directions
Imaging
Inferring
Predicting/confirming
Synthesizing

AGE GROUP
All ages

Once you've modeled the process of interacting with text, your students need a chance to practice for themselves with your guidance. That's where Teacher Task Cards come in.

Getting Ready

1. Copy the reproducibles for task cards on pages 14–20 onto 8½" x 11" colored card stock.
2. Laminate the copies.
3. Cut the sheets into individual cards.
4. Punch a hole in the corner of each card and put the cards on a 1" book ring.
5. Place the cards in a spot where they'll be readily available for you to use with students.

The Process

1. Look at books with the students.
2. Follow the instructions on the task cards. This gets the children used to interacting with the text.

TEACHER TIP
Note that the task cards can be used with all kinds of books—fiction and nonfiction, picture books and chapter books. The same skills apply to all of these, and these task cards give students a great way to practice them.

MATERIALS
• Correction tape
• Sticky notes (3" x 5")
• Lap boards (if available)

Teacher Task Cards for Think-Alouds

Look at the cover.

Show the children the cover of the book and get them talking about it by using these questions: **"What do you think the book will be about? Who might be the characters? What might happen?"**

PREDICTING

CONNECTING WITH PRIOR KNOWLEDGE OF STORY ELEMENTS

Name the story.

Discuss what makes a good book title (e.g., it's short, gives information about the story, intrigues you to read it). Select an unfamiliar book and cover the title of the book with correction tape. Say, **"After reading the story, talk with your partner about possible titles for the story."**

JUDGING IMPORTANCE

Draw a quick sketch.

Choose an unfamiliar book and cover the illustration on the cover with construction paper. Make sure each child has a piece of paper and a thin-line marker. Use lap boards if you have them. Reveal only the name of the book. Say, **"Sometimes the title of a book can give us a lot of information. But sometimes we get even more information from the illustration that is on the cover of the book. I've covered up the cover illustration, so I want you to look at the title of this book. What do you think the story might be about? What might happen in the story? I'm going to give you one minute to sketch a picture of what you think the story might be about."**

INFERRING (what we already know)
PREDICTING (what we think we'll find out)

Look at the back cover.

Read the story description. Say, **"Now we have more information. Can we add to or change our book prediction?"**

PREDICTING (refining previous predictions)

"Read" the illustrations.

Say, **"Book illustrators (or artists) help us to get more from the story. Let's try to tell the story from the pictures first."**
Take a "picture walk" through the book by looking at the illustrations. Stop and talk about book characters, setting, events.

PREDICTING STORY ELEMENTS

Guess the word.

Use a big book or a chart story. Before reading the story, go to the second or third line of the story's text and cover a key word with correction tape. Read the story to that point and then ask the students, **"What word might make sense in that spot?"** Take one of the words they suggest and write it on a sticky note. Read the sentence again, inserting the word from the card. Ask, **"Does it make sense?"** Do this with a couple more words. Then reveal the first letter of the actual word in the story's text. Say, **"Now you see the first letter. What word might make sense that starts with that letter?"** Generate more words for the sticky notes. Finally, uncover the whole word and check the students' predictions against it.

USING FIX-UP STRATEGIES

Identify story elements.

Choose one story element: character(s), setting(s), events, problem, or solution. Read the book with that one element as your focus. Reread the same book at another time for a different element. Say, **"Today as we read, we're going to look for the _____ of the story. When we're through reading, be ready to _____ (talk about, draw, or write about) the story's _____."**

JUDGING IMPORTANCE

What would you ask?

Choose an unfamiliar short story. Say, **"Good readers are always asking questions as they read. Sometimes the author answers the questions and sometimes the author gives hints about the answers. As we read today, we'll stop at each page and make a list of questions for the author. We'll check to see if the answers are found in the book or if we have to develop our own answers from what we already know."**

QUESTIONING

INFERRING

CONNECTING

Create pictures in your head.

Select a book with few or no pictures. Make sure each child has a piece of paper and a thin-line marker—preferably a marker that's a dark color, because dark colors are easier to see. Use lap boards if you have them. Say, **"Authors use special words to help us make a picture or even a movie of the story in our own heads. Today, we will stop and draw quickly what the author helped us see in our heads. Be listening and imagining what the author is telling us about."** Stop at key points, each time allowing one minute for each student to do a quick line drawing. Then have each student share her drawing with a partner and tell about the words that helped make her "mind picture."

IMAGING

First, last, and mostly about

Say, **"As we read today, be listening for how the author begins the story and how the author ends the story."** After discussing this information as a group, ask students to turn to their partners and explain what they think the story is "mostly about."

JUDGING IMPORTANCE

Keep it going.

At the end of the story, decide with your students how the author could continue the story. Ask, **"Would the characters change in some way? How about the setting? The problem? Could there be a new solution to the problem?"**

QUESTIONING
PREDICTING
INFERRING

Nonfiction: learning and questioning

Pick a nonfiction book—perhaps one that is relevant to a topic you are currently studying or getting ready to study. Make sure that each child has a piece of paper and a pencil. Use lap boards if you have them. Gather the students in your reading area and say, **"Nonfiction is something that is true. As we read today, I'll stop after each page and we will make a list of new things we've learned, and a list of questions that we have for the author of the book."**

QUESTIONING
CONNECTING

Questions for the experts

Some of the students' questions may not have been answered in the book as you read along. Decide where else you could look for those answers or who else you could ask. Set tasks for inquiry. Make a chart of questions the class has. For each question, list who is assigned to find the answer, and sources they can try. As students come back with answers they were able to find, add those answers to the chart. Continue filling in the chart over the course of several days, adding more questions, assignments, sources, and answers as they come up.

QUESTIONING
CONNECTING

Student Task Cards for Think-Alouds

After you have modeled Teacher Think-Alouds in your classroom, give students an opportunity to practice thinking aloud with partners. While you're reading, stop and allow students to think about the different story elements or text features. This gives you the opportunity to observe and assist selected pairs of students.

Getting Ready

1. Copy the reproducibles for task cards on pages 22–26 onto 8½" x 11" colored card stock, laminate the copies, and cut the sheets into individual cards.
2. Punch a hole in the corner of each card and put the cards on a 1" book ring.

The Process

1. Get out your selected text, place these Student Think-Aloud Cards in your lap, and start reading the text.
2. When you reach an appropriate "stop and talk" place in your story, choose one card and pose to the class the question on the card. Use this question as a springboard for discussing the text.
3. Ask each student to turn to someone near him to discuss the answer to the question.
4. After a few moments of discussion, listen to selected pairs to assess if any students need additional guidance.
5. Now pair up children who are reading the same book, and give each pair a laminated and ringed set of task cards.
6. After they finish reading a section of the book, have each pair choose one card from the set. Ask them to respond to that question as they discuss the section of the book that they have just read.

PURPOSE
To improve reading comprehension

INTELLIGENCES
On-my-own learner
With-friends learner
Word learner

LEARNING STYLES
Auditory learner
Visual learner

GROUP SIZE
Pair or triad
Individual

SKILL
Problem-solving

AGE GROUP
All ages

TEACHER TIP
Not every card is appropriate for every group. Which ones you choose will depend on the group's maturity and experience with this type of "text talk."

Student Task Cards
for Think-Alouds

Did any part of this book puzzle or confuse you? Are you asking yourself any questions about the book?

What did the author say in the story that made you want to turn the page and keep reading?

If the characters in the story were sitting next to you, what would you like to ask them?

4

Does the book remind you of another book that you have read? Explain.

5

Did the setting of the story remind you of a place you have been? Explain.

If you were writing the story, what changes might you make in it?

Do any of the characters remind you of someone you know? Explain.

8

What part of the book did you like the most?

9

What part of the book did you dislike? Why?

READING ACROSS THE CURRICULUM
Overview

One of the hallmarks of differentiated instruction is a focus on engaging and motivating individual students by addressing each child's unique interests and abilities. A language arts program that uses the differentiated approach finds a way to capture each child's interests and imagination by "reaching him where he lives"—encouraging him to read and write about the subjects that interest him and to develop specific language arts skills as he practices them across the entire curriculum.

This section explains how to plan a unit of study that will take into consideration your students' gifts and interests. It also gives you a framework for gathering readily available resources that you can use in your classroom to expand the understanding of your students.

Planning a Literacy Cluster

A literacy cluster is a series of activities that stretch across multiple disciplines, allowing students to make connections and to understand how the concepts they're learning are relevant to a specific topic or area of interest. In other words, they help students to learn.

Getting Ready

1. Choose your theme. As you decide on the topic to be studied, keep in mind the individual interests, abilities, and intelligences of your students. Let's say that your unit of study is going to be about flight.

2. Expand the topic. You might take a field trip to an airport or ask a pilot to come to speak to the class.

3. Provide reading material appropriate for the different reading levels, interests, and intelligences of your students. One child might need a book at a reading level different from that of the rest of the class; another child might be intrigued by reading about the Wright brothers; a child who is spatially oriented will benefit from a book with illustrations showing how to construct and fly several different designs of paper airplanes. You direct more accelerated students to learn about flight manuals or to search the Web for information.

4. Provide other materials as well. Offer videos for children who respond best to that kind of presentation.

5. Provide time for sharing. When the students have explored the topic, have them share their discoveries with the class. This expands the knowledge of all the students at many different levels.

6. Decide on the "essential ideas" of your theme. These are the big ideas that you want your students to take away from this study and retain. In this case, the essential ideas might be:
   a. Flying has fascinated man for centuries (that's the historical perspective).

b. The principles of flight have challenged science and spawned many experiments, trials, and successes, as well as failures.

c. Problem-solving drives imagination, skills, and growth.

7. Plan how you could use a still broader variety of materials to create a literacy cluster around this theme. Think of the materials already available to you in your classroom and the school library. What Web sites might help students to learn more about this theme? Will they be able to get relevant information from the local newspaper? What magazines could be useful? Who in the community might be an expert on this subject? Could students interview that person? Collect the actual materials or draw up a list of available resources for your students.

8. Make a copy of the Literacy Cluster Planning Grid on page 31. Fill in the copy with actual book titles, page numbers, Web sites, and names of local experts.

TEACHER TIP

Think about how the activities you're choosing will address the standards of your state and the expectations of your district. If your district requires that the students "read in a variety of genres," you want to be sure that you make available not only fiction and non-fiction, but also poetry and some nonstandard pieces of literature (brochures, flyers, other media pieces).

Literacy Cluster Planning Grid

Theme: _Critters_

Essential Ideas: _Insects have 3 body parts, 6 legs • Arachnids (spiders) have 2 body parts, 8 legs • Habitat/diet differences • Life cycle/time line differences_

	Source Name	Page #s	Essential Elements/ State Standard	Notes
TEXTBOOK	Science Basal	20	The student knows that living organisms need food, water, light, air, a way to dispose of waste, and an environment in which to live.	Look for subheading in Ch. 3 about living organisms.
TRADE BOOKS	Spiders by Gail Gibbons		Student can identify characteristics of living organisms.	Use directed listening/thinking activity to compare different spiders.
MAGAZINE	Ranger Rick		Student can compare and give examples of the ways living organisms depend on each other and on their environments.	Use current issue to compare insects' habitats.
NEWSPAPER	Kids' page from local newspaper		Student demonstrates an understanding of informational text in a variety of ways.	Use recent copy to create an informational web about spiders.
LOCAL EXPERT	Joe Jones, local pet-store owner		Student obtains information about a topic using a variety of oral resources such as conversations and interviews.	Invite Mr. Jones to class; ask him to bring spiders.
INTERNET	www.google.com www.askJeeves.com www.yahooligans.com		Student reads from a variety of genres to acquire information from both print and electronic sources	Search for "arachnids."

9. Make a copy of the Sample Tasks grid on page 32 and fill it in with ideas for what your students can produce using the information they gather.
10. In the classroom, set up stations where children can complete these tasks.

The Process

1. Encourage students to go to more than one area during the time you're devoting to this theme.
2. As students complete the tasks, assess their progress based on what they produce.

Sample Tasks

Reading/Writing	Compare two or more books on the theme.
Math	Compare the different parts of a spider. Create a graph showing different habitats of spiders.
Paired Study	Choose an insect that you and a friend would like to learn more about. Decide which books and/or resources will give you unique information, and investigate them.
Research (Solo)	Choose an insect that you would like to learn more about. Decide which books and/or resources will give you unique information, and investigate them.
Poetry/Music	Create your own lyrics to an original or familiar tune. Look for some additional poetry relating to insects. Be ready to share with the rest of the class.
3-D Model	Create your own insect. Name your insect and label the various parts.
Theater	Create a Reader's Theater on "The Life of an Insect." (Go to www.aaronshep.com for a free download that explains how to create a Reader's Theater.)
Artistic	Paint or draw an insect. Label your insect and add a caption to give more information to your readers.
Additional student options:	

Literacy Cluster Planning Grid

Theme: _____

Essential Ideas: _____

	Source Name	Page #s	Essential Elements/State Standard	Notes
TEXTBOOK				
TRADE BOOK				
MAGAZINE				
NEWSPAPER				
LOCAL EXPERT				
INTERNET				

Sample Tasks

Reading/Writing
Math
Paired Study
Research (Solo)
Poetry/Music
3-D Model
Theater
Artistic
Additional student options:

Choices for Literacy Activities

The Record of Literacy Activities provides a simple, clear way for children to record their choices and for you to monitor their literacy activities. The form is designed for an older elementary classroom set up with individual workspaces.

Getting Ready

Make one copy of the reproducible on page 36 for every student in the class.

The Process

Ask each student to choose any option on the schedule. After she completes that task, tell her to write the completion date in the appropriate row and column of her chart. (If she chooses "Taped Book Activity" on Monday, January 14, then she would write "1/14" in the first block in that row of the chart.) Then ask her to choose an activity from any other section. Tell her that she must complete every other activity before repeating any. So if on Monday she also completes "Radio Reading," on Tuesday she won't be able to go back to either "Radio Reading" or "Taped Book Activity" until she has completed an activity from every other section.

The exception to the "no repeating" rule is "Independent Book Reading." Students don't necessarily have to complete other activities before returning to this one. The independent reading option is always available to every child; after all, you are trying to build your students' reading stamina.

The "Teacher Conference" section also works a little differently from the rest of the chart. In this case, the difference is that the conference isn't a choice; it's required. Teachers need to take regular opportunities to check in on the "status of the student" to assure that each child is completing the work and choosing options at the appropriate level for his abilities. Explain to students that the goal is for the teacher to meet

MATERIALS
- Computer
- Book-reading programs for computer
- Tape player
- Prerecorded audio tapes of books
- Tape recorder
- One blank audiotape per student
- Response sheet for "Radio Reading" (see page 37)

with each student at least once during the week, and that the conference needs to take place before the student repeats any activities (other than independent reading). A child who feels the need to meet with the teacher more often is welcome to ask for extra conference time.

Definitions of Literacy Activities

Independent Book Reading: Student chooses an appropriate book and reads it on her own. She then chooses one of the task cards for

Radio Reading

Names of partners   Jacob

Christopher

Name of book/literature being recorded
"The Silver Fish"
(poem by Shel Silverstein in <u>Where the Sidewalk Ends</u>)

List sound effects that would enhance the reading and when to use them

Sound effect:	Page/place to use sound:
Splashing water	At the beginning – set the scene
Dropping/clinking coins	"Palace of gold"
"Kerplunk"	"I threw him free"
Ha-ha-ha-ha (hysterical)	"He laughed at me"
Splashing water	"I caught the fish again"
Sizzling sound	"He was delicious"

Date to be shared   10/14

Teacher approval   *Mrs. VanderWeide*

reading log responses (see pages 137–49), and responds to the instructions on that card by writing in her reading journal.

Making Books: Student completes a piece of creative writing or writes a story that is a variation on something he's read. Then he makes his creation into a multipage booklet with a cover.

Computer Reading: *This doesn't mean computer games!* Student reads book text (e.g., Living Books) on a computer.

Taped Book Activity: Student listens to prerecorded audio tapes while following along in the printed text. These tapes can be ones that go with library books or they can be specially paced tapes for children who need support in their reading.

Buddy Reading: Child reads a book with a partner, and then works with that partner to respond to questions from a task card they choose together (see pages 104–10).

Radio Reading: In this paired activity, children choose a story and decide together what sound effects (e.g., splashing water, footsteps, laughter) would enhance the experience of listening to the story. They list their ideas (using a copy of the form on page 37), and then record the story together, incorporating sound effects.

Poetry Cards: The teacher creates an enlarged copy of a poem that children would enjoy reading, and then mounts the enlarged copy on a 9" x 12" sheet of construction paper. Underneath the poem, the teacher writes instructions for an activity the child is to complete (e.g., write another poem like this one, or pick out three interesting words in the poem that made you want to reread it).

Teacher Conference: Child brings her reading journal to a meeting with the teacher. Together, student and teacher examine responses and look at the types of books that the child is reading.

TEACHER TIP

The supplies column in the Literacy Activities chart is a reference for both the student and the teacher. It's the teacher's responsibility to be sure the necessary tools are ready and available. It's the child's responsibility to use the supplies column as a checklist and be sure he has everything he needs to complete the activity he's chosen.

Once students begin completing their charts, they need a place to store them. Reading Response Folders (see pages 130–68) are the perfect spots for this.

Sample Literacy Schedule

(for an 80-minute literacy block, allowing 10 minutes for transition time)

- Arrival and homework check-in. Independent reading or partner work. (5 minutes)
- Whole-group read-aloud or modeling lesson. (20 minutes)
- Literacy activities choices (30 minutes)
- Group sharing of literacy activities work progress (15 minutes)

Record of Literacy Activities

Center	Monday	Tuesday	Wednesday	Thursday	Friday	Supplies
Independent Book Reading (with journal response)						• Book • Journal • Writing materials
Making Books						• Paper • Scissors • Art materials
Computer Reading						• Computer program for reading • Journal
Taped Book Activity						• Taped book • Tape player • Journal
Buddy Reading						• Book • Sticky notes • Art paper (for graphic organizers)
Radio Reading						• Book • Tape recorder • Blank tape • Response sheet
Poetry Cards						• Poetry card or book • Journal
Teacher Conference						• Book • Reading journal

Radio Reading

Names of partners _____

_____

Name of book/literature being recorded

_____

_____

List sound effects that would enhance the reading and when to use them

Sound effect:	Page/place to use sound:

Date to be shared _____

Teacher approval _____

Coded Bookmarks and Flags

PURPOSE
To help students focus and prepare to discuss the text

INTELLIGENCES
On-my-own learner
On-the-move learner
With-friends learner
Word learner

LEARNING STYLES
Auditory learner
Tactile/kinesthetic learner
Visual learner

GROUP SIZE
Small group (4–6)
Pair or triad
Individual

SKILLS
Comparing/contrasting
Creative expression
Evaluating
Fix-up strategies
Following directions
Imaging
Inferring
Predicting/confirming
Problem-solving
Questioning
Synthesizing

AGE GROUP
Older

While students are reading on their own, reading bookmarks and sticky notes keep them focused on the reading tasks set for them. The bookmarks show students what to look for (e.g., something they don't understand, something that is new information, or an impressive turn of phrase). The sticky notes give them a way to mark the exact spots in the text to which they want to refer back. These simple devices also prepare students to share with others those parts of the text that were meaningful to them and that they would like to discuss.

Getting Ready

1. Turn to the reproducible bookmarks on pages 40–43. Choose the one(s) most appropriate for the reading your students will be doing (not every child in the class will need every type of bookmark). You'll need bookmarks only for the children with whom you are working in small groups.
2. Add to the bookmarks any other codes that you feel will be useful in the lessons you're planning.
3. Copy the reproducible(s) onto colored card stock, using a different color for each version of bookmark. Don't laminate the bookmarks; you want your students to be able to write on them.

The Process

1. Give each student a bookmark that's appropriate for his skills and for the way he learns best, along with a few strips ("flags") cut from sticky notes.
2. Ask your students to add to the bookmarks any other codes that will be meaningful to them.

3. Tell them that as they read, each child should look for the kinds of things listed on her bookmark. When she finds something that's on her bookmark, she should write the appropriate code from the bookmark on one of her sticky "flags," and place the flag at the exact spot in the text (or next to an illustration or caption) that made a special connection for her. This allows the student to focus on something she wants to call to the attention of fellow students during "after-reading talk time." It also sets a task for early finishers and gives them a purpose for rereading while waiting for the other students.

4. Have students share with the rest of the class the text (or illustrations or captions) they've marked.

MATERIALS
• Sticky notes (3" x 3"), cut into shorter strips

VARIATION

For younger students:

Skip the bookmarks, but have the children use the sticky "flags." If you're working with emerging readers, give two sticky "flags" to each student. Instruct each child to mark one place in the book that was interesting and one place where he had a problem. You don't need to label the "flags"; children are able to remember the two choices. The sticky "flags" keep the talk focused on the text, the illustrations, and the problem-solving that good readers do as they negotiate text.

Codes for Sticky "Flags"

!

? Didn't understand word or part of story

PS Problem solved (I figured it out)

S Surprised

W What great words!

T I need to Talk to someone about this part

Codes for Sticky "Flags"

!

? Didn't understand word or part of story

PS Problem solved (I figured it out)

S Surprised

W What great words!

T I need to Talk to someone about this part

Codes for Sticky "Flags"

!

? Didn't understand word or part of story

PS Problem solved (I figured it out)

S Surprised

W What great words!

T I need to Talk to someone about this part

Codes for Sticky "Flags"

!

? Didn't understand word or part of story

PS Problem solved (I figured it out)

S Surprised

W What great words!

T I need to Talk to someone about this part

2

Codes for Sticky "Flags"

I Important

R Reminds me of something I already know

MP Mental Picture

! Inference (I used what I know and added new information)

P Prediction

C Confirmed my prediction

2

Codes for Sticky "Flags"

I Important

R Reminds me of something I already know

MP Mental Picture

! Inference (I used what I know and added new information)

P Prediction

C Confirmed my prediction

2

Codes for Sticky "Flags"

I Important

R Reminds me of something I already know

MP Mental Picture

! Inference (I used what I know and added new information)

P Prediction

C Confirmed my prediction

2

Codes for Sticky "Flags"

I Important

R Reminds me of something I already know

MP Mental Picture

! Inference (I used what I know and added new information)

P Prediction

C Confirmed my prediction

3 Nonfiction

☆ I already know this

+ New information

! Wow! Great writing!

?? I don't understand

---

3 Nonfiction

☆ I already know this

+ New information

! Wow! Great writing!

?? I don't understand

---

3 Nonfiction

☆ I already know this

+ New information

! Wow! Great writing!

?? I don't understand

---

3 Nonfiction

☆ I already know this

+ New information

! Wow! Great writing!

?? I don't understand

Codes for Sticky "Flags"

D Descriptive language

I Instructional language

? Unsure of the meaning (word or passage)

S Solved my problem

W Wow! Great writing

N Need to talk to someone about this part

Codes for Sticky "Flags"

D Descriptive language

I Instructional language

? Unsure of the meaning (word or passage)

S Solved my problem

W Wow! Great writing

N Need to talk to someone about this part

Codes for Sticky "Flags"

D Descriptive language

I Instructional language

? Unsure of the meaning (word or passage)

S Solved my problem

W Wow! Great writing

N Need to talk to someone about this part

Codes for Sticky "Flags"

D Descriptive language

I Instructional language

? Unsure of the meaning (word or passage)

S Solved my problem

W Wow! Great writing

N Need to talk to someone about this part

ENERGIZERS
Overview

Two especially wonderful aspects of the differentiated classroom are the energy and creativity that are released as students work together to solve problems and generate ideas. For that reason, it is appropriate, in this look at differentiated instruction, to include Energizer activities that emphasize student collaboration—the process in which two or more students work together to define a task or gather more information.

The idea behind collaboration is that students must listen carefully to each other in order to build new understandings and to clarify their thoughts about a subject or piece of literature. The collaboration process almost always produces more thinking than could be generated by students working alone. Besides, collaboration can also be a great way to engage and motivate students.

When collaboration takes the form of Energizer activities like the ones in this chapter, you get the benefits of collaboration *and* an opportunity to:

- ◆ get your students on their feet and their minds in gear
- ◆ have children move around the classroom and interact with each other in a purposeful activity
- ◆ let students share information and clarify their thinking—as you guide them to reach your objectives for the lesson

In short, Energizer activities offer a great way to prepare your students for some creative thinking that's both exciting and unusual. They'll love them, *and* they'll learn from them.

The Open-Ended Response Board

This simple, quick activity is a great way to introduce kids to thinking creatively and organizing their thoughts. Use the Response Board to generate and gather a lot of ideas from your students about a particular topic or subject area. Then help them to organize those ideas into natural groupings.

Introduce the Concept

1. Explain to your students that this is a way to gather and organize a lot of ideas about a particular topic.
2. Tell them that all ideas will be accepted.
3. Explain that after they've listed their ideas, the class will work together to organize and label those ideas. Note that this is a good way to develop a comprehensive understanding of a topic.

Set Up the Workspace

1. Hang the large piece of butcher paper low enough so that students can reach it.
2. Give each student a marker and three or four sticky notes. Explain that more are available if students need them.

Identify the Topic

1. Choose a topic with a broad definition that will encourage multiple responses (e.g., "community," or, for younger children, "friendship").
2. Introduce the topic to the class as you write it on the board. You might start out with a statement like, **"Think about what you already know about this place you live in"** or **"What does the word 'community' mean to you?"** Be careful not to say too much. If you overdo it, you'll narrow responses as your students try to fit in with your stated parameters.

PURPOSE
To stimulate creative thinking

INTELLIGENCES
With-friends learner
Word learner

LEARNING STYLES
Auditory learner
Tactile/kinesthetic learner
Visual learner

GROUP SIZE
Whole class

SKILLS
Categorizing
Creative expression
Organization
Problem-solving

AGE GROUP
All ages

MATERIALS
- Large sheet of butcher paper
- Sticky notes (3" x 5")

Generate Ideas

1. Instruct students to think about what they already know about the topic you've named, and to write each thing they know on a separate sticky note.
2. Remind the class that all ideas are to be accepted without discussion.
3. Have students stand and read their notes, one at a time.
4. After reading what he's written, each child gets to stick his note anywhere on the butcher paper.
5. Collect about eight responses (you want to stimulate their thinking, not exhaust it).

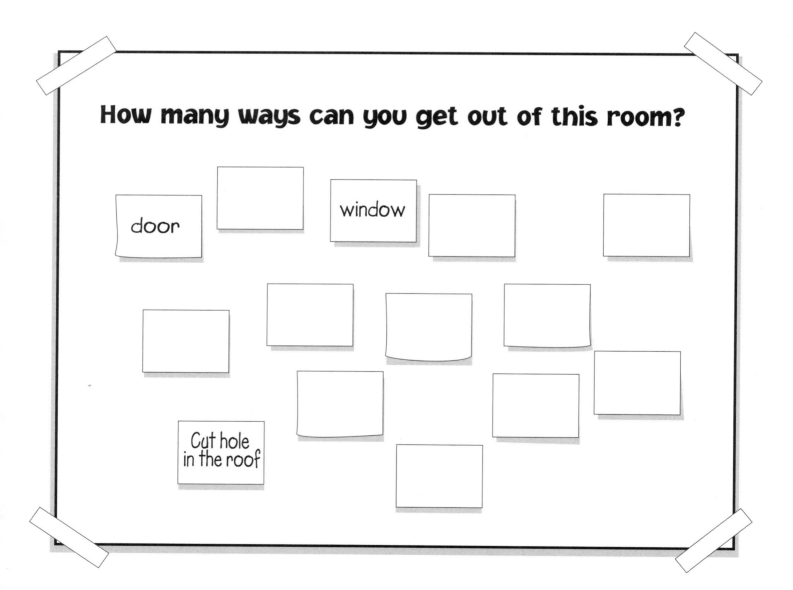

How many ways can you get out of this room?

door

window

Cut hole in the roof

VARIATIONS

For small groups:

Use 12" x 18" construction paper to create a smaller Response Board for each pair or triad. Write the focus question on the chalkboard. Have each small group respond to that same question by recording their responses onto smaller (3" x 3") sticky notes and placing them on their own Response Board. Now, have each small group take blank sticky notes and go "shopping for ideas." Instruct each group to go around the room and read the ideas that are on the other groups' Response Boards. If they see an idea that they like, they can copy it onto a sticky note and add it to their own Response Board. This incorporates the important skill of evaluation into the process; the students have to evaluate the other responses to determine whether those responses are appropriate to the topic. This usually takes less than five minutes. Then have each group return to their own Response Board and incorporate the newly "purchased" ideas. Now have them group and label the responses, just as with the whole-group activity.

For older students only:

Ask students to respond in their journals to the same open-ended question that was on the classroom Response Board. Encourage any student who's having trouble with spelling or terminology to borrow a note from the Response Board, copy the troublesome word into her journal, and then return the sticky note to the board. This supports the child who has difficulty copying from the board.

Clarify for Understanding

1. Have students discuss any unclear ideas.
2. Encourage students to ask questions for clarification, and to keep those questions positive. ("Could you explain that to me?" "Could you give me an example?").
3. Remind students that this is a time for clarifying, not for agreeing or disagreeing.
4. Help students rephrase any negative comments. ("That makes no sense" might become "What are you trying to say?") To keep the discussion positive, you may want to make copies of the posters on pages 179–80 ("Ways to Say More When You Agree" and "What to Say When You Disagree") and refer your students to these posters prior to and during the discussion.

Group the Related Ideas

1. Have students take turns going to the wall and rearranging ideas based on the natural relationships of those concepts.
2. Take on the role of facilitator (asking questions that will stimulate connections), rather than that of director (showing students the correct answer).
3. To be sure everyone understands and agrees with the groupings, periodically stop and have the students discuss their ideas as a group.
4. Continue the categorizing process until all are satisfied with the emerging categories.

Create Categorizing Titles

1. Determine logical titles for each category.
2. Based on the class's input, prepare another sticky note for each category title and place it above the appropriate group of sticky notes (or have older students do this themselves).

Nonfiction Thinking and Reasoning

PURPOSE
To activate prior knowledge and help children make connections

INTELLIGENCES
Nature learner
Number learner
On-my-own learner
On-the-move learner
With-friends learner
Word learner

LEARNING STYLES
Auditory learner
Tactile/kinesthetic learner
Visual learner

GROUP SIZE
Whole class
Small group (4–6)
Pair or triad
Individual

SKILLS
Categorizing
Comparing/contrasting
Inferring
Organization
Predicting/confirming
Questioning

AGE GROUP
All ages

The concept of the Response Board (see pages 45–48) provides a jumping-off point for building vocabulary. Then use a chart to activate prior knowledge before reading a nonfiction book together.

Getting Ready

Prior to the lesson, choose 10 to 20 vocabulary words from a nonfiction book that the class will be exploring. (The number depends on the age and maturity of the children.) Ideally, try to choose words that (a) may be difficult for the children; (b) are key terms to the area of study; and (c) aren't obviously associated with the book's topic. That last piece gives you a chance to reinforce the concept that one word may have multiple meanings, and to expand the list of potential associations students can make. If you were working on *Meet the Octopus* by Sylvia James, your choices might include the words "beak," "crabs," "enemies," "eggs," "dwarf," "giant," "funnel," and "babies."

Day 1

1. Write each word on a separate sticky note.
2. Place one word on the butcher-paper Response Board. Tell students that the word appears in the book they're going to be reading, and ask them to suggest any other words or concepts that are related to that word. As they do this, they're inferring what the book might be about. If the initial word were "eggs," for example, students might infer that this will be a book about birds. They might respond orally with "birds," "snakes," "cake," or "scrambled."
3. Add more words, one at a time, asking for associated words or concepts to go with each addition. You might put up the word "babies" so they know the topic is not "cake" or "scrambled."
4. Next, you might put up the word "beak." That eliminates snakes, so students begin to see that this might be a book about birds.

MATERIALS
• Response Board
• Sticky notes (3" x 5")

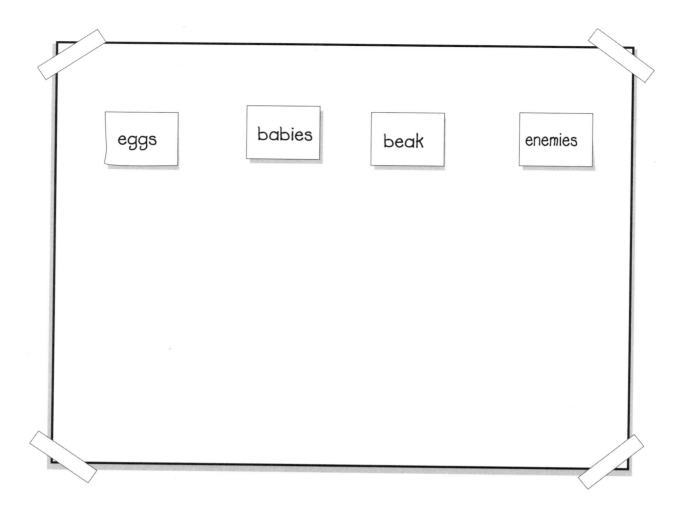

5. Have each student turn to a partner. Say to the class, **"What connections are these terms making in your head? Discuss these connections with your partner. Are your thoughts changing? How? Or are the additional terms agreeing with your original thoughts? How?"**

6. After all the words are on the board, ask a volunteer to choose any two or more words from the Response Board and create a sentence using those words. Using "crabs," "enemies," and "babies," the sentence could be "Crabs are enemies of the babies." The student doesn't have to write this down. He can just say his sentence for the class.

7. Ask another volunteer to create a different sentence from the words on the board—choosing some of the same words used by the first child, if he wants, or all different ones.

8. If you like, repeat the process one more time, just to be sure the students get the idea.

9. Place the sticky notes with these words in an area of the room where children can have access to them, and encourage children to continue making as many sentences as they can from them. Tell them that in each sentence, they need to connect at least two of the words.

Day 2

1. Bring back the sticky notes with the vocabulary words from Day 1.
2. Show students the title of the book you're exploring together, the table of contents, and the index. Explain that the table of contents groups concepts into categories, and that the index of the book gives you an alphabetical listing of the terms.
3. Identify 3–4 categories that are related to the book's topic. For *Meet the Octopus,* those categories might be "protection," "enemies," "habitat," and "food." Write the name of each category on a sticky note and place all of the sticky notes on the Response Board.
4. Have the students name 3–4 words or phrases that reflect their understanding of the book's topic. Write these on sticky notes, too, and have the students determine which of the words or phrases should be placed under each of the categories you've listed. In this case, students might say that "suckers," "arms," and "ink" should be placed under "protection." Some of the words they identify may be from the activity on Day 1, and some may be from their prior knowledge. Some may be misconceptions, but do not correct them; you're still allowing for discovery. At this point, the students are connecting their thoughts from Day 1 to their understanding of the topic ("octopus").

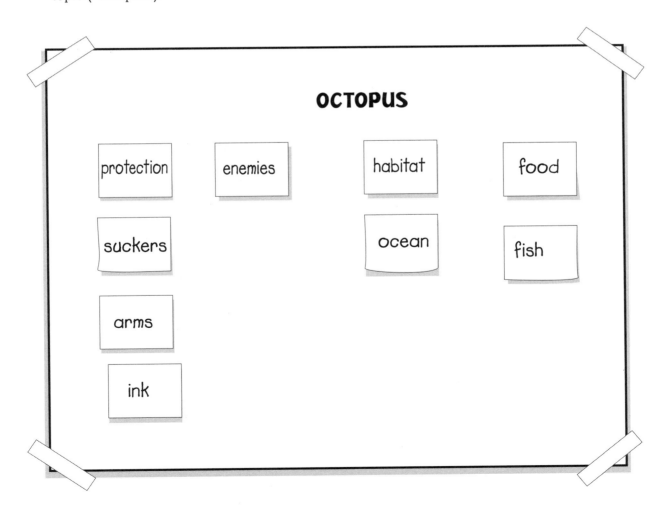

5. Now it's time to move on from vocabulary to the larger concepts of the book. On the board, create a KWL chart. A KWL chart has three columns. Label the first column "What We Think We Know." Label the second column "What We Want to Know." Label the third column "What We Learned."

6. As you write down the responses, have students brainstorm together to fill in the first two columns of the chart. By using the terminology they've been working with already, they're activating their prior knowledge and preparing to learn more.

Day 3

1. Read the book to the class, and then go back to the Response Board.

2. Together, check what the students have written and how they've grouped the terms they were working with.

3. Return to the KWL chart and fill in the third column together.

Anchor Charts

During whole-group brainstorming activities, you can use graphic organizers to record student contributions and to arrange those thoughts in logical groupings. The charts you create together then become "anchor charts"—models that students can reference later as they construct their own organizers. If your classroom has limited wall space, try replicating these charts in a spiral easel chart or a smaller spiral notebook, and then placing those samples in an area of your classroom that is accessible to your students.

Web

Use webs to make connections among key ideas. Place the main topic or idea in the middle of the paper, and then connect that central idea to subtopics (written on 3" x 5" sticky notes) with lines or arrows. You can use words and/or pictures for each concept. For each note, try to gather four responses based on prior knowledge. Be sure to call on different students so that you gather different perspectives and get many responses.

PURPOSE
To model for students multiple ways to organize their thinking

INTELLIGENCES
Number learner
With-friends learner
Word learner

LEARNING STYLE
Visual learner

GROUP SIZE
Whole class

SKILLS
Categorizing
Comparing/contrasting
Creative expression
Imaging
Inferring
Organization
Sequencing
Synthesizing

AGE GROUP
All ages

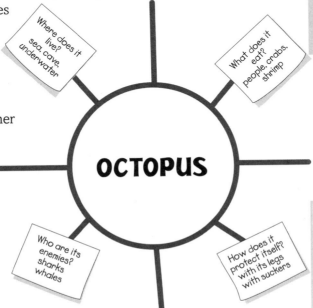

Where does it live? sea, cave, underwater

What does it eat? people, crabs, shrimp

OCTOPUS

Who are its enemies? sharks whales

How does it protect itself? with its legs with suckers

MATERIALS
• Manila paper (12" x 18")
• Sticky notes (3" x 5")

Story Map

The story map is a variation on the web; use this approach to identify the elements in a story. Be sure to leave plenty of room for students to fill in their responses.

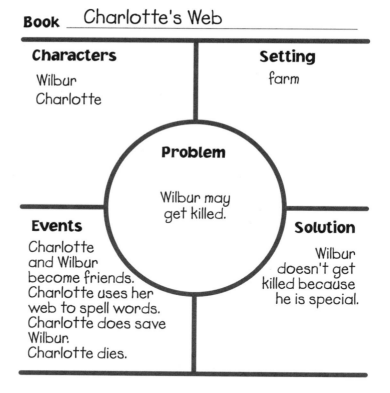

Book Charlotte's Web

Characters
Wilbur
Charlotte

Setting
farm

Problem
Wilbur may get killed.

Events
Charlotte and Wilbur become friends.
Charlotte uses her web to spell words.
Charlotte does save Wilbur.
Charlotte dies.

Solution
Wilbur doesn't get killed because he is special.

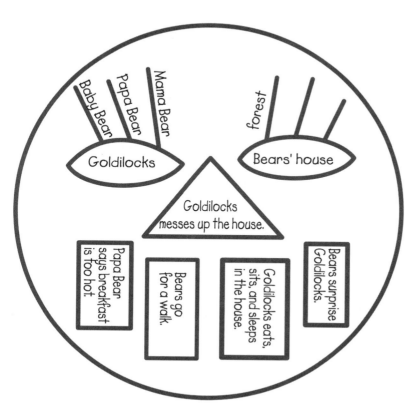

Story Face

Use story faces to help children identify the main character and main setting in the book they're reading. Instruct students to label the elements of the story face as follows …

Left eyeball: name of the main character

Eyelashes on that side: names of other characters

Right eyeball: name of the main setting

Eyelashes on that side: names of other settings

Nose (for trouble): the central problem in the book

Each tooth: an event from the book

Have the children decide whether it's a happy story or a sad story, and arrange the "tooth" boxes in a smile or a frown accordingly.

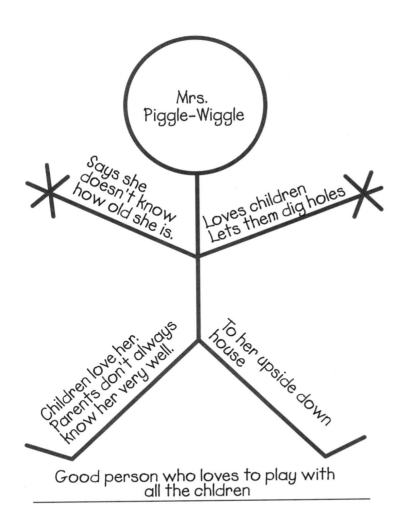

Mrs. Piggle-Wiggle

Says she doesn't know how old she is.

Loves children Lets them dig holes

Children love her. Parents don't always know her very well.

To her upside down house

Good person who loves to play with all the chldren

Character Stick Person

Character stick people offer a good way to build reading comprehension of a book with a strong central character. Following the illustrated model (based on *Mrs. Piggle-Wiggle,* by Betty MacDonald), instruct children to label the blanks as follows …

For the head, draw a picture of the main character's head or write her name.

On one arm, write what the character does that is special.

On the other arm, write what she says that makes her different.

On one leg, write where she goes.

On the other leg, write what other people think of her.

On a line under the person, write a sentence telling what kind of person she is.

Frayer Model

This chart is a great way to reinforce understanding of vocabulary words. To make a Frayer Model, tell students to follow these steps:

1. Draw a large square and divide it into four equal parts.
2. Draw a large circle in the middle of the four squares.
3. Put a vocabulary word in the circle.
4. In the top left box, write a definition of the word in your own words.
5. In the top right box, write what the word isn't.
6. In the bottom left box, write an example of how you might apply the word.
7. In the bottom right box, give an example of something the word doesn't apply to.

If you're working with younger children, substitute pictures—suggested by the children—for the words in the boxes.

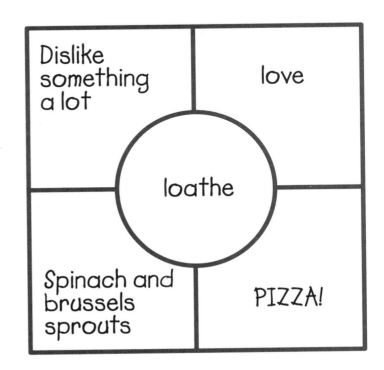

Dislike something a lot

love

loathe

Spinach and brussels sprouts

PIZZA!

```
1998                          2001    2002    2003
 ●                             ●       ●       ●        ●
I was born.                   My family  We got   I started
                              moved to   a new   kindergarten
                              Boston.    puppy.
```

Time Line

Use this organizer with material that has a chronological sequence.
Instruct students to follow these steps:

1. Draw a line from left to right across the center of the page.
2. Place one dot on the line for each major event being studied.
3. Write the appropriate year (or day or month) above each dot.
4. Under each dot, write the event that happened at that time.

Two-Column Notes

This is a good approach to analyzing reading material that's especially challenging. Following the model illustration (based on Madeline L'Engle's *A Wrinkle in Time*), tell students to:

1. Draw a line down the center of the page from the top to the bottom.
2. On the left side of the page, write a quote from the text you are reading that causes you to stop and question or think.
3. On the right side, opposite the quote, write down your questions or your wonderings about what the author has written.

Meg says; "Like and equal are not the same thing at all."	How are they different? What does that mean? A chicken can be like a robin, but they are very different.

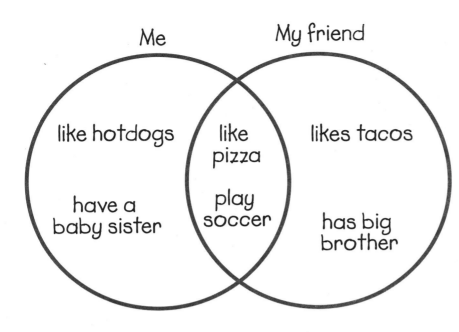

Me   My friend

like hotdogs

have a
baby sister

like
pizza

play
soccer

likes tacos

has big
brother

Venn Diagram

Use this organizer to show how two things are alike and/or different. Tell students to:

1. Draw two large circles that overlap, creating three large spaces for writing.
2. At the top of each circle, write the name of one of the two things you are comparing.
3. In the circles' overlapping segment, write how the two things are alike.
4. In the outer segments, write what is unique about each term.

Three-Circle Map

This is a way to summarize a story using three separate circles. Following the sample (based on *What Will Little Bear Wear?* by Else Holmelund Minarik), model this process for the class:

1. Draw two unconnected circles, one in the top left corner and one in the top right corner of the paper.
2. In the left circle, write or draw how the story started.
3. In the right circle, write or draw how the story ended.
4. Draw a third circle under and between the first two. In this third circle, write or draw what the story was mostly about.

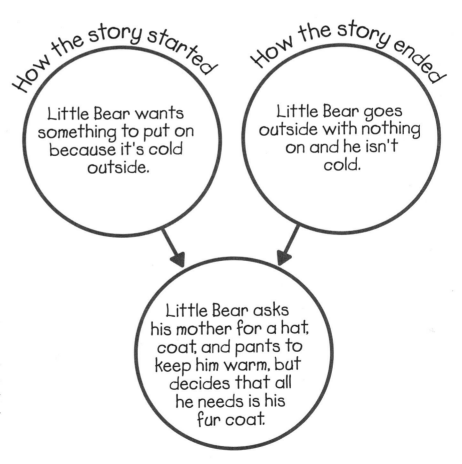

How the story started

Little Bear wants something to put on because it's cold outside.

How the story ended

Little Bear goes outside with nothing on and he isn't cold.

Little Bear asks his mother for a hat, coat, and pants to keep him warm, but decides that all he needs is his fur coat.

What the story was mostly about

Vocabulary Mapping

This organizer helps a student to define how things are categorized and what attributes they have. Tell the child to take a sheet of paper and:

1. Halfway down the left side of the paper, draw a rectangle.
2. In that rectangle, write the name of an animal or another item that can be categorized.
3. Starting at the top of the rectangle, draw a line up toward the top of the page.
4. At the top of the line, draw another rectangle.
5. In this second rectangle, write the classification of the animal or item (e.g., bird).
6. On the right side of the paper, make three boxes, one under the other.
7. Draw a line from each box to the first rectangle.
8. In each of the three boxes, write one way to describe the animal.
9. On the bottom of the chart, draw three more boxes with lines to the first rectangle.
10. In these boxes, write "kinds of" or "uses for" the original word (e.g., "emperor," "king," "fairy").

What I liked	What I didn't like
I liked the wild things.	Max being in trouble

Questions I have	Connections I'm making to other things
Did it really happen or was it a dream?	Reminded me of Pinocchio because he got in trouble. Reminded me of a time I got sent to my room, too.

Tell Me Questions (Movie Exit Questions)

These are the questions people ask as they leave the theater. They also make great questions to use immediately after reading a story. Following the model (based on *Where the Wild Things Are,* by Maurice Sendak), tell each student:

1. Divide your paper into four sections.
2. In the top left section, answer the question, "What did you like?"
3. In the top right section, answer the question, "What didn't you like?"
4. In the bottom left section, answer, "What questions do you have?"
5. In the bottom right section, answer, "What connections are you making to other things?"

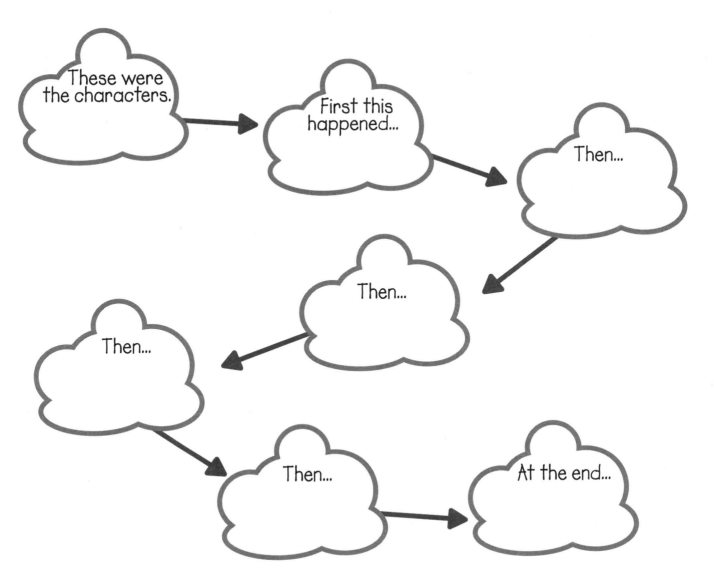

Story Sequence Map

These picture-and-arrow maps work with all ages.

1. Start at the top left of the paper and draw a quick sketch of the characters in the setting where the story begins.
2. Put a "cloud" around the picture.
3. Draw an arrow to the right, and draw the next event in the story.
4. Put another "cloud" around this picture.
5. Continue drawing each event and using arrows to show a left-to-right sequence until you get to the edge of the paper.
6. When you get to the edge, make the next arrow point down.
7. Draw the next event on the right side of the paper.
8. Draw arrows and pictures from right to left until you reach the left side of the paper.
9. Continue the zigzag pattern of arrows and pictures down the rest of the page, until the pictures come to the end of the story and the final event.

Tools for Creative Thinking

PURPOSE

To model divergent thinking, stimulate creative brain-storming, and encourage students to apply those techniques to the writing process

Creative thinking epitomizes the whole philosophy of differentiated instruction, recognizing that "We are different learners who learn and think differently." Creative thinking builds on the concept that a single question can have multiple answers. When you challenge students to produce alternative responses, stressing that there are no *wrong* answers, you support any child who otherwise may be hesitant about joining in. When you reward the out-of-the-ordinary response, you build a sense of community; every child feels a part of the group. Besides, when you encourage creative or divergent thinking, you also invite students to respond with a sense of humor, and humor is a wonderful "brain break" (opportunity to assimilate information) in any situation. These Creative Thinking Tools are sure to bring smiles to your classroom.

So, how do you teach creative or divergent thinking? One approach is to break it down into its component parts. To get students thinking creatively, try modeling some of the key components of good writing: fluency, flexibility, originality, elaboration, and evaluation. (You can probably come up with other components as well, but these will get your students started.) Let's consider how we might define each of those pieces, and how you can model each one for your students.

Fluency is the ability to think of lots of responses to a single prompt or question. **"How many different ways can you say 'said'? 'Nice'? 'Pretty'?"** It's like developing a thesaurus in each student's mind. You're asking the students to think of answers that are really subsets of the main category. "Told" or "spoke about" or "reported" are all answers that fit within the broad category of alternatives to "said."

Flexibility means the ability to shift thinking from one way to another, to look at things from another point of view. **"How would a minor character in this story view the main character? What would the story be like in a different setting? What would happen if the problem changed? If the solution changed? If events changed?"** Fluency involves thinking of subsets; flexibility involves thinking of alternatives.

Originality involves coming up with responses that are clever, unique, and relevant—but not obvious. Try asking students to go back to stories they've written and consider whether changing the circumstances of a particular story would result in a different outcome. **"What kind of animal might this person be? Would effect would that have on the story? What planet could this take place on, and how would that change things?"**

Elaboration requires adding details to a basic idea to make it more interesting and complete. **"How could you change a three-word sentence by adding more adjectives or adverbs? How can you take this simple sentence and make it more intriguing, interesting, memorable?"**

Evaluation means weighing the desirability of alternative ideas. Whether it's in the context of a book they're reading or their own writing, ask the students: **"Which word would be better to describe this character? Which is more interesting? Which reveals more? Which suits the purpose better?"**

Once your students understand the basic components of creative thinking, there will be no stopping them! To give children a chance to apply these new skills in other situations, turn to Goldilocks Thinking Tools on the following pages.

TEACHER TIP

Highly verbal children will excel in this area. This doesn't mean, however, that other types of learners won't be able to respond. They might just need a little more time to think.

After posing your prompt or question, allow some Think Time (5 to 8 seconds). Don't allow any oral responses during this Think Time. This gives everyone a chance to formulate a response before you begin recording them. Make sure that you allow *additional* Think Time—it can be later in the day—after you describe to students what you want them to do.

Goldilocks Thinking Tools

If you take the same Creative Thinking Tools discussed in the preceding pages and apply them to literature, you give your students a whole new way to explore and remember what they have read. At the same time, you'll encourage them to add an extra twist to their own writing process.

Introducing the Activity

When introducing these strategies to your class, it's a good idea to start by applying them to a story that is already familiar. That way, your students aren't struggling to remember details, but instead can concentrate on looking at an old story in a new way. Let's use "Goldilocks and the Three Bears" as an example. Here is a great way to take that old favorite to a whole new level.

The Process

For the fluency, flexibility, originality, and evaluation exercises, all you need to do is write the headings and instructions from the following pages on class charts, and then add to the charts over several days. You can act as scribe, writing directly on the charts as younger children contribute their ideas, or you can let older students write their suggestions on sticky notes and post the notes on the charts themselves. Either way, try to get at least eight responses for each of these four categories.

The elaboration exercises—the picture stretcher, story stretcher, and setting stretcher—are slightly different. Use the picture stretcher with a pair or a group of no more than four children. The story stretcher is good for small groups, and children can complete the setting stretcher independently. All they'll need from you is a model to get them started.

Note that you'll probably want to leave out the words in italic when you create the story stretcher and setting stretcher charts for your students. If they're stuck for examples, though, get them started with these.

Questions for Fluency Exercises

What might Goldilocks see in the three bears' house?

Where might the bears go on their walk?

What mistakes did Goldilocks make?

Name other things that come in threes.

Questions for Flexibility Exercises

List all the kinds of breakfasts the bears might have left for Goldilocks to taste.

List all the different kinds of chairs Goldilocks could have sat on.

List all the kinds of beds Goldilocks could have slept in.

Draw how Goldilocks would have looked to Baby Bear if she had fallen asleep in his tree house; in his wagon; in his pajamas.

Questions for Originality Exercises

How could the bears have kept Goldilocks out of the house?

What could Goldilocks have done instead of exploring the house?

What could Goldilocks have done besides running away?

Question for Evaluation Exercise

Are you for or against Goldilocks going into the bears' house? Write your name in either the "For" or the "Against" column. Then explain your reasoning in the "Why" column.

Elaboration Exercises for "Goldilocks"

Story Stretcher

Begin your story.	"Once upon a time, there was a ——— girl named Goldilocks."
Now, add one word to describe her.	Little
Continue adding descriptive words until you have several.	blonde, chubby, nosey, tall, crabby ...

Setting Stretcher

What other parts of the house could Goldilocks have gone to?	And what would she have done there?
Closet	Tried on clothes
Bathroom	Used the bears' toothbrushes
Attic	Tried the bears' old furniture

Picture Stretcher

If you're the person starting this chart, draw Goldilocks wearing a simple dress that she might have worn on that day. Now pass the picture to someone else in your group. The next person to get the picture should add one more thing to the outfit. Continue passing the picture and adding to it until the group is satisfied that it's complete.

Goldilocks

Thinking Strategies for Readers

Once students have learned the five creative thinking strategies outlined on pages 60–61, and have applied them to a familiar story like "Goldilocks," the next step is to use those same strategies to strengthen their comprehension of new material. Here are some sample exercises for students. Although these examples are designed for use with the book *Best Friends,* by Steven Kellogg, you can adapt them to work with other books as well.

To address fluency

Have students make a bulletin board listing books about friends. Instruct children to include each book's title and author, and a drawing to show what the book is about.

To address flexibility

Ask each student to list or draw the things she and her friends like to do together that are different from what the characters in *Best Friends* do.

To address originality

Say to your students, **"Write about the feelings of the different friends in the book. Then tell about a time when you felt the same way. When was that, and what happened?"** Encourage students to respond in unexpected ways.

PURPOSE
To encourage students to use the Creative Thinking Tools in their study of literature

INTELLIGENCES
On-my-own learner
Word learner

LEARNING STYLE
Visual learner

GROUP SIZE
Whole class
Individual

SKILLS
Categorizing
Comparing/contrasting
Evaluating
Following directions
Organization

AGE GROUP
All ages

My Friend

One character in the book feels like her friend has found a new friend. She is jealous of this new friend. I felt the same way when my best friend, Sarah Jane, invited someone else to spend the night instead of me. That was two weeks ago, and my feelings were hurt. But then my mom reminded me that sometimes I ask other friends to do things, too. Sarah Jane can still be my best friend, but it's okay to have other friends.

Funny
Runs fast
Asks lots of questions
New to our class
Knows big words

To address elaboration

Have each student think of one of his best friends. Tell him to write the letters of that person's name down the side of a piece of paper. On each line, he should write a word or phrase that describes the friend and includes the letter from his name. For example, if the friend is named Frank, the student might write "Funny" on the first line.

Happy Times
My birthday
Her birthday
Trip to playground

Sad Times
My goldfish died
Our friend Amanda
moved away

To address evaluation

Friends experience both fun and difficult times together. Have each student make a chart with one column for happy times and one column for sad times. In the column for happy times, ask the child to draw or write about happy experiences she's shared with a friend. In the column for sad times, she should draw or write about sad times they've experienced together.

The Bulletin Board That Grows

PURPOSE
To encourage flexible thinking, fluency, and originality

INTELLIGENCES
Nature learner
Word learner

LEARNING STYLES
Tactile/kinesthetic learner
Visual learner

GROUP SIZE
Whole class

SKILLS
Categorizing
Creative expression
Organization

AGE GROUP
Younger

The global thinker or less verbal child can be a part of this activity; it doesn't matter if he gets his "Aha!" later in the day or even the next day. Children who need more time to respond can still contribute when the idea strikes. An added bonus: The longer the chart stays up, the more original the responses become!

Getting Ready

1. Cover your bulletin board with Kraft paper in a bright color that's appropriate for the current season—perhaps orange in October, white in January, or red in February.
2. Leave room for a title at the top; then section off the rest of the Kraft paper into approximately 10 spaces, using a marker or colored masking tape.

Activity

1. Choose an object that's appropriate for the current month—you might use an apple in September or a pinecone in December.
2. Hand the object to a child, and ask the child to describe one attribute of the object (attributes for an apple might include "hard," "cold," "red," "shiny," "sweet").
3. Write that attribute on a sticky note in one of the spaces on the bulletin board. Let's assume the child says "red."
4. Have the child pass the object to the next person, and ask that child to either name a different attribute or pass the object on while he thinks. Explain that each attribute must be unique—no repeats!
5. If this child describes the apple as "shiny," you write the word "shiny" on a sticky note in its own separate square, and the student passes the object to the next person.

(continued on page 69)

MATERIALS
- Brightly colored Kraft paper
- An object that's seasonally appropriate
- Sticky notes (3" x 5")

APPLE

RED Fire truck Crayon	SHINY Penny Daddy's shoes	SWEET Soda Candy My mom		

Items to Try

Certain seasonal objects work especially well for this exercise. These are some of my favorites for each month of the school year.

September	apple
October	pumpkin
November	turkey feather
December	pinecone
January	ice cube
February	candy box
March	"gold" coin
April	egg (make sure it's hard-boiled!)
May	flower

6. If a child who has asked for thinking time is ready to contribute, go back and get his contribution.

7. After filling in the chart with approximately 10 descriptive words, it's time to move on to the next step. Go back to the first square (in this case, the one that says "red"). Ask the children to think of a different object that has that same attribute (for "red," it might be "fire truck" or "crayon").

8. As children generate other ideas, you or the students write or draw each response on a sticky note, and then place the note in the square where the original attribute ("red") is written. Only new ideas are allowed in each square—again, no repeats!

9. Once you've built the basic chart, encourage students to come back to it over several days. Tell them to add to the squares as they think of new things that have the same attributes. This is when you'll see the most creativity!

VARIATION

For older students:

When you section-off the bulletin board, create 20 spaces rather than 10. Choose a more complex object such as "The Earth." Show the students a picture of the object and then have the students list its attributes: They might describe the atmosphere, earth layers, inhabitants, etc. They can add to the bulletin board throughout your unit of study, following the same basic process as the one for younger students.

Asking Questions with More than One Answer

PURPOSE

To encourage students to ask creative questions that invite multiple responses

Every day in our classrooms, we ask lots of questions. "What was Lincoln's first name?" "How do you spell this word?" "What are the names of the characters in this story?" Those are "reproductive" questions. When we ask a reproductive question, we're asking students to "reproduce" a rote answer. The question is very literal, requires convergent thinking, and calls for a single answer. Five times two will always be ten, no matter how many times we ask the question.

But what if we ask different kinds of questions? "Why did people call Lincoln 'Honest Abe'?" "What other words can you think of that contain this sound?" "What would be different about this story if it took place on the moon?" These are "productive" questions. Productive questions allow for open-ended possibilities and multiple answers; they require divergent thinking. These are the questions that open students' minds to creative thinking. There are many equations in which the answer is ten.

Reproductive Questions	Productive Questions
Where are the doors in this room?	What are all the ways you can get out of this room?
How long does it take you to walk to school?	What are all the ways you can travel to school?
What are the parts of a clock?	What are all the ways to use a clock other than as a timepiece?
What three important things happened in Humpty's story?	What are ways to put Humpty Dumpty back together again?
What are the names of the original 13 colonies?	What are some of the names that might have been given to the 13 colonies if the first colonists had landed on Los Angeles Rock? (Remember, the Pacific coast was controlled by the Spanish!)

Creating Productive
Questions

To introduce your class to the differences between the two types of questions, you need an activity that models for them how to turn reproductive questions into productive ones. This activity is designed to do just that.

The Process

1. Take the "reproductive" questions on page 70 and write each one on a separate sentence strip.
2. Place one strip at the top of your Response Board.
3. Distribute the sticky notes to the students. Have the students split up into pairs, and instruct each pair to write on a sticky note a "productive" version of the reproductive question on the sentence strip.
4. Ask students to read aloud their "juicy" questions and add them to the Response Board.
5. After all questions are on the board, have each pair of students come up and remove a sticky note written by someone else.

PURPOSE
To reinforce creative thinking and creative questioning

INTELLIGENCES
On-the-move learner
With-friends learner
Word learner

LEARNING STYLES
Auditory learner
Tactile/kinesthetic learner
Visual learner

GROUP SIZE
Small group (4–6)
Pair or triad

SKILLS
Comparing/contrasting
Fix-up strategies
Problem-solving
Questioning

AGE GROUP
Older

MATERIALS
• Sentence strips
• Sticky notes (3" x 5")
• Response Board (see pages 45–48)

6. Ask the student pairs to return to their seats and discuss the two versions of each question (the "reproductive" question on the sentence strip and the "productive" question on the sticky note). Once both students have answered both versions of the questions aloud, the pair should write down all of their answers, using the following sample chart. Encourage students to notice the marked difference not only in the length of the answers to the two types of questions, but also in the quality and diversity of the responses.

Reproductive Question	Productive Question
How long does it take you to walk to school?	What different ways can you travel to school?

7. Now it's time to return to the whole group. Ask the students to share with the class their experiences with the reproductive and productive questions. Which caused them to think and to talk more?

8. Repeat the process with other sentence strips, until you're sure that students have mastered the concept.

Using Productive Questions to Study Literature

PURPOSE
To boost reading comprehension by reviewing literature with open-ended questions

INTELLIGENCES
With-friends learner
Word learner

LEARNING STYLES
Auditory learner
Visual learner

GROUP SIZE
Pair or triad

SKILLS
Comparing/contrasting
Following directions
Questioning
Synthesizing

AGE GROUP
All ages

Once the students have a basic understanding of the differences between reproductive and productive questions, it's time for them to apply what they've learned to literature.

Getting Ready

1. Make two copies of the reproducible on page 74 for each student in your class.
2. Make one more copy on an overhead transparency.

The Process

1. Review with your students the differences between the two types of questions, and explain that now it's their turn. They get to change their own "reproductive" questions into productive questions.
2. Distribute the paper copies of the reproducibles to the students.
3. To model for students how they can turn reproductive questions into productive ones, place the transparency on an overhead projector. Work with the students to fill it in together.
4. Divide the class up into pairs of students, making sure that both students in each pair are currently reading the same book.
5. Have the pairs repeat the process you've modeled, applying it to the book each pair has read.
6. Monitor each pair's progress to be sure they understand the process.

Reproductive and Productive Questions

Name Carter

Name of book _Magic Tree House #3 Mummies in the Morning_ Author _Mary Pope Osborne_

1. Think about the book that you and your partner are currently reading.

2. Make a list of reproductive questions you would expect to be asked about the book's details. Write your questions in the left column.

Questions	Answers
Where does Annie think Jack would like to go?	Egypt
What did Jack write in his notebook?	"coffin called sarcophagus"
Who is Hutepi?	Queen of the Nile

3. Now change the questions so that there is more than one possible answer. Write your new questions in the left column.

Questions	Answers
Why are the Magic Tree House books unique or special?	Annie and Jack visit lots of fun and interesting places and people. They also get to travel in time, which is cool. I learn a lot.
If you saw a mummy in Egypt what questions would you ask it?	How did you die? Was there lots of gold? Did you eat bugs?
How would you describe Hutepi?	Really gross looking—rotting away

4. Exchange papers with your partner and answer each other's questions.

5. What do you both notice about the amount of talking and thinking each type of question generates?

Reproductive and Productive Questions

Name _____

Name of book _____ Author _____

1. Think about the book that you and your partner are currently reading.

2. Make a list of reproductive questions you would expect to be asked about the book's details. Write your questions in the left column.

Questions	Answers

3. Now change the questions so that there is more than one possible answer. Write your new questions in the left column.

Questions	Answers

4. Exchange papers with your partner and answer each other's questions.

5. What do you both notice about the amount of talking and thinking each type of question generates?

I've Got the Answer! Who's Got the Question?

This takeoff on *Jeopardy* is something students love. It starts from a model the kids know (the television game show), but unlike the show, this game encourages multiple responses and plenty of creative thinking.

The Process

Begin by modeling on the board just how the process works—perhaps using some of these examples. In each case, write the "answer" on the board, and then encourage all the creative "questions" the kids can come up with. If they get stuck, you might lead them to some of the responses listed below.

**"The answer is 'pop'!
Who's got a question?"**
What is the name of the sweet, fizzy stuff that comes in a can?
What do we sometimes call Dad?
What do people do with balloons?

**"The answer is 'furry'!
Who's got a question?"**
How does a rabbit feel?
What do your teeth feel like in the morning?

**"The answer is 'reptile'!
Who's got a question?"**
How are a crocodile and a snake the same?
What animal that's alive today is closely related to the dinosaur?

The answer is "pop"!

The answer is "furry"!

The answer is "reptile"!

PURPOSE
To teach students how to ask questions

INTELLIGENCES
On-the-move learner
With-friends learner
Word learner

LEARNING STYLES
Auditory learner
Tactile/kinesthetic learner
Visual learner

GROUP SIZE
Whole class

SKILLS
Categorizing
Creative expression
Organization

AGE GROUP
All ages

MATERIALS
• Sticky notes

Once the children understand the process, they can continue it on their own. Write a new answer and post it on the bulletin board. Encourage students to respond over several days by writing their questions on sticky notes and placing them on the bulletin board underneath the answer. Typically, kids love the progressive nature of this activity and enjoy reading each other's responses. Change the "answer" heading every few days.

PREVIEW AND REVIEW GAMES
Overview

Activating prior knowledge—previewing—gets your students ready to learn. Practice and review cement new skills into long-term memory. These preview and review games give your students a chance to practice essential skills together and to have fun at the same time.

The Move and Match Cards in the following pages are designed primarily for older students. For your younger learners, you might want to try making your own—slightly different—Move and Match Cards. Try asking younger students to match:

◆ picture cards with cards showing the initial sounds of those pictures
◆ picture cards for words that rhyme
◆ picture cards and word cards

Note that because these activities can be completed pretty quickly, they also work well as a way to get kids into pairs or groups of three for some other activity.

Dictionary Move and Match

Use the Dictionary Move and Match Cards to familiarize your students with terms that they will encounter when using a dictionary. This game uses two sets of cards: one for Dictionary Game Terms and a second for Dictionary Game Definitions. Each term has two definitions. There are 24 cards, so you may need to adjust for your class size, setting aside some of the cards or adding more as needed.

Getting Ready

1. Before class, copy the Dictionary Game Terms from page 80 onto one color of card stock and copy the Dictionary Game Definitions from page 81 onto a different color of card stock.
2. On the back of the card stock, code the terms and their corresponding definitions for easy checking.
3. Laminate both sets of cards and cut them apart.

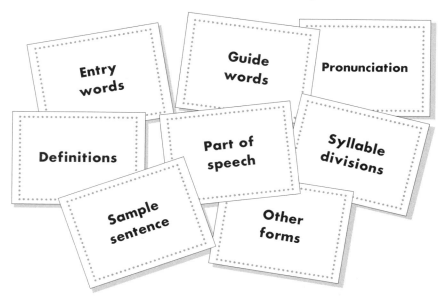

To Play

1. In class, give one card to each student.
2. Have students walk around the room to locate the cards that go with theirs. If you use all the cards, you should end up with groups of three students, each group holding one term card and two definition cards.
3. Have students switch cards with students from different groups and play again.

EXTENSION

Once the children are comfortable with the terms and definitions, have students write their own definitions of the terms. Use these cards for the next go-around of the game.

Dictionary Game Answer Key

Definitions

1. List all possible meanings of the word
2. Help you find the right meaning for your word, as shown by the context

Entry words

1. Are the words being defined, listed alphabetically
2. Let you check a word's spelling and capitalization

Guide words

1. Tell the first and last word on that page
2. Help you find the word you want

Other forms

1. List related forms of the word
2. Show spellings of related words

Part of speech

1. Tells whether a word is a noun, verb, adverb, and so on
2. Helps you use a word properly in a sentence

Pronunciation

1. Shows how you should pronounce, or say, the word
2. Helps you learn how to say the word

Sample sentence

1. Is a sentence that shows the word in context
2. Shows how to use the word

Syllable divisions

1. Are shown with a space or heavy dots that separate syllables
2. Help you check how to divide a word into syllables or at the end of a line of writing

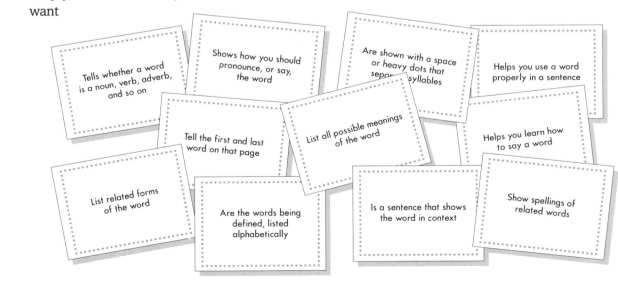

Dictionary Game Terms

Pronunciation	Guide words
Part of speech	Entry words
Other forms	Definitions
Syllable divisions	Sample sentence

Dictionary Game Definitions

Help you find the word you want

Let you check a word's spelling and capitalization

Help you find the right meaning for your word, as shown by the context

Shows how to use the word

Helps you learn how to say a word

Helps you use a word properly in a sentence

Show spellings of related words

Help you check how to divide a word into syllables or at the end of a line of writing

Tell the first and last word on that page

Are the words being defined, listed alphabetically

List all possible meanings of the word

Is a sentence that shows the word in context

Shows how you should pronounce, or say, the word

Tells whether a word is a noun, verb, adverb, and so on

List related forms of the word

Are shown with a space or heavy dots that separate syllables

Nonfiction Move and Match

Nonfiction has its own vocabulary and identifying features. When you're introducing (or even "reintroducing") nonfiction, it's helpful for your students to have a working knowledge of these elements. Use these cards to remind students of what they should be looking for as they begin their journey into nonfiction.

Getting Ready

1. Before class, copy the reproducibles on pages 84–85 onto card stock.
2. On the back of the card stock, code the terms and their corresponding definitions for easy checking.
3. Laminate each full page, and then cut the cards apart. There are 20 cards, so you may need to hold some back or add extra copies to adjust for the size of your class.

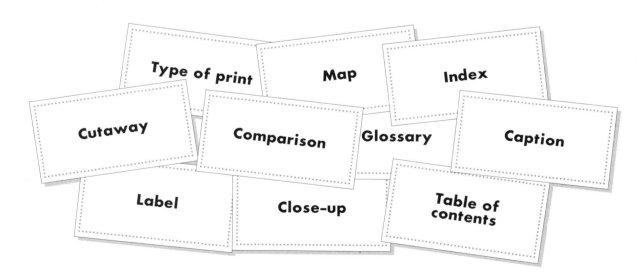

To Play

1. Give each child a card.
2. Have students move around the room, matching terms and definitions. If you use all the cards, you should end up with 10 pairs of students.

Nonfiction Move and Match Answer Key

Caption: I help the reader better understand a picture.

Close-up: I help the reader see something small.

Comparison: I help the reader to understand the size of something by showing it next to an object that's familiar.

Cutaway: I help the reader by showing something with the outer layer (like a wall) removed.

Glossary: I help the reader by defining the words in the text.

Index: I am an alphabetical listing of almost everything in the text, with page numbers for reference.

Label: I help the reader identify the parts of a photo or illustration.

Map: I help the reader understand where things are in the world.

Table of contents: I help the reader identify the key concepts in the book in the order they are presented.

Type of print: I help the reader by signaling key topics in the book with different fonts.

Nonfiction Move and Match Cards

Type of print	**Label**
Close-up	**Glossary**
Table of contents	**Map**
Index	**Cutaway**
Caption	**Comparison**

Nonfiction Move and Match Cards

I help the reader by defining the words in the text.

I help the reader understand where things are in the world.

I help the reader identify the parts of a photo or illustration.

I help the reader by showing something with the outer layer (like a wall) removed.

I help the reader by signaling key topics in the book with different fonts.

I help the reader better understand a picture.

I help the reader see something small.

I help the reader identify the key concepts in the book in the order they are presented.

I help the reader to understand the size of something by showing it next to an object that's familiar.

I am an alphabetical listing of almost everything in the text, with page numbers for reference.

Goldilocks Rap

MATERIALS
• Poster board (22" x 28")

This activity provides another opportunity for kids to get up and get moving with a purpose. Use the "Goldilocks Rap," a fun version of "Goldilocks and the Three Bears," to introduce this active form of learning.

You can also create your own cards using text from other sources. Using cards for a "line-up review" reinforces communication skills and enhances sequencing skills and memory. Because the children work together and everyone shares the responsibility of "telling" the story, all your students will benefit from this exciting approach to learning.

Getting Ready

1. Before class, use the enlargement feature on the copier to copy the reproducible on page 87 onto a sheet of 11" x 17" paper. Then copy and enlarge once more, this time using card stock. This will give you two large sheets of card stock and will make the individual cards a convenient size.
2. Laminate the card stock, and then cut the cards apart.
3. Make another copy of the reproducible on plain paper, again enlarging it twice. Mount the paper copies on poster board.

To Play

1. In class, using the poster board copy for reference, recite this rap with your students. Together, add fun actions, motions, and voices.
2. Distribute the cards, giving one to each student.
3. Randomly ask each student to read his card aloud.
4. As they are reading their cards, have students begin to arrange themselves in the order of the rap. Have them decide who goes first, next, and so on. Let the students solve this together as a collaborative effort.
5. Once they're in order, have students recite the entire rap again, following the correct sequence.

TEACHER TIP
This exercise is designed for 20 students. If you have 21 students, make an extra card with the title; for 22 students, add one more that says "The End." Have 23? Assign the role of "assistant" to a child without a card. Have the assistant help any child who is having difficulty reading his card or determining where he belongs in the order.

If you have fewer than 20 students, all the students can say the first and last cards together. Also, everyone can say "Ba, ba, ba-ree bear," because everyone thinks it's fun!

Goldilocks Rap Cards

Once upon a time,
in a nursery rhyme,
there were three bears.
I said three bears.

One was the Papa Bear.

One was the Mama Bear.

One was the Baby Bear.

Then, down through the forest
came a walking, talking,
pretty little Goldilocks.

And upon the door she was
a-knocking.
(Knock, knock, knock)

No one was there. Uh-oh.
No, no one was there.

So she walked right in.

Yes, she walked right in.

She didn't care!
Uh-uh, she didn't care!

Then, home, home, home
came the three bears.

"Someone's been sitting in my chair,"
said the Papa Bear.

"Someone's been sitting in my chair,"
said the Mama Bear.

"Ba, ba, ba-ree bear,"
said the Little Wee Bear.

"Someone has broken my chair!"
Crash!

Then Goldilocks woke up,
broke up the party,
and beat it out of there.

"Good-bye, good-bye, good-bye,"
said the Papa Bear.

"Good-bye, good-bye, good-bye,"
said the Mama Bear.

"Ba, ba, ba-ree bear,"
said the Little Wee Bear.

This is the story
of the three bears.
Yeah!

Toss to Twelve

Rote learning is necessary for some material, but you can still differentiate. In this game, students at different levels work with different vocabulary lists but share the same game.

Getting Ready

1. Divide the poster board into 12 equal sections. Number the squares from 1 to 12. Laminate the board.
2. On one index card, write the easiest 12 vocabulary words. Number them from 1 to 12.

MATERIALS
- Poster board (22" x 28")
- Small beanbag
- Peel-off stickers in two colors
- Six index cards (5" x 8"), unlined

3. Repeat for each additional card, using progressively more difficult terms. If you use all 6 cards and put 12 words on each, that gives you a total of 72 words.

4. Assign each card a letter that represents its degree of difficulty, and write the letter on the back of the card. This allows you to match each student with the words that are at the appropriate level of difficulty.

VARIATION

For a change of pace: Follow the same steps, but ask students to define the words or to use them in a sentence.

To Play

1. Pair off the students.

2. Give each student a vocabulary card (if the paired students are at the same reading level, they can share a card) along with a set of 12 stickers. Each child's stickers should be a different color from her partner's.

3. Set the poster board on the floor.

4. Have students take turns tossing the beanbag onto the board.

5. Tell the students that the student who tossed the beanbag is to take the number from the square that the beanbag landed on and find the corresponding number on his vocabulary card. He should then try to read the vocabulary word that is next to that number. If the beanbag falls on a square for which the student already has a sticker, the child loses that turn and the beanbag goes to the other student.

6. If the student can read the word, he puts a sticker in his unique color on the section of the poster board where the beanbag landed. If he cannot read the word, his partner can help him, but then he doesn't get to put a sticker on the board. (The next time the beanbag lands on that square, the child must be able to read the word without help.)

7. The first person to have a sticker in each of the 12 squares on the board wins the game.

8. At the end of the game, students remove their stickers from the board and place them on scrap paper to take home.

Walk-on Shower Curtain

MATERIALS
- Six clear sheet protectors (8½" x 11")
- Clear shower curtain liner
- Clear, 2"-wide mailing tape
- 48 index cards (5" x 8"), unlined
- One *lightweight,* plain paper plate (9")
- Large paper clip

To Prepare the Shower Curtain Liner

1. The goal is to create pockets on the shower curtain liner.
2. Cut each sheet protector into four pieces, each 5½" x 8½".
3. Place the shower curtain liner on the floor.
4. Space the sheet protector pieces evenly across and down the shower curtain liner, creating six rows with four pieces in each row.
5. Use the clear mailing tape to secure the pieces to the shower curtain liner on the sides and bottom of each piece, leaving the top of the piece open.
6. Insert an index card into each pocket. These are your "space holders"; they help you to see the pockets when you're replacing old playing cards with new ones for a new round of the game.

To Prepare the Playing Cards

1. On each of the other 24 index cards, write one piece of information you want the children to review. This might be a single word, a phrase, or a question (e.g., "Define 'Exoskeleton'"; "Give a prepositional phrase"; "Name the 13 original colonies"; "Who's the main character in *Charlotte's Web?*").
2. Insert one playing card in each pocket of the shower curtain.

To Prepare the Spinner

1. With a ruler and a marker, divide one of the paper plates into quarters.
2. Number the sections from one to four.
3. Laminate the plate so that it will hold up during repeated game playing.

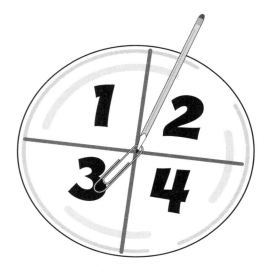

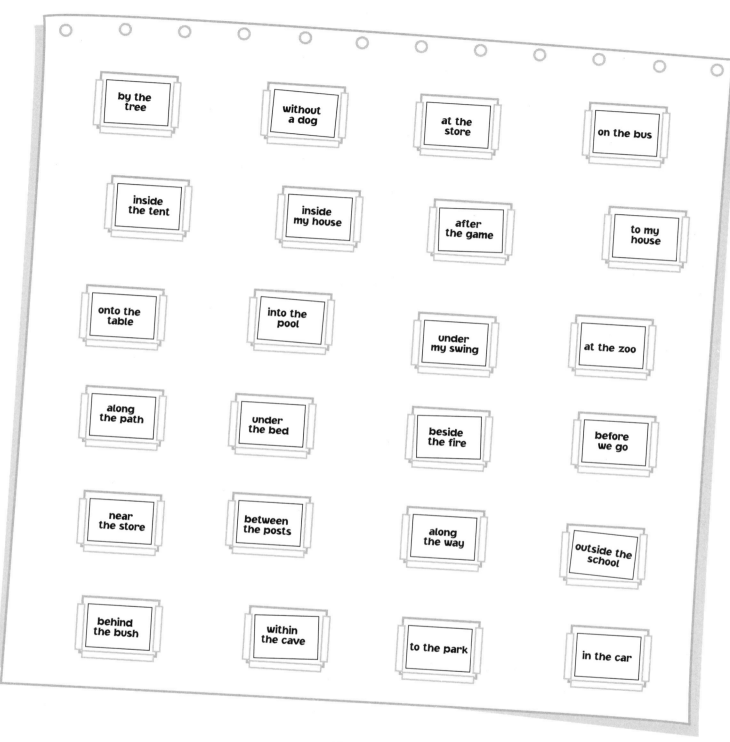

In this version of the Walk-on Shower Curtain, you'd instruct each student to move the number of spaces indicated by the spinner. Then the child should stop, read the phrase he's landed on, and use the phrase in a sentence. Each time he moves to another space, he must come up with a new sentence about a new topic.

To Prepare the Draw Cards

1. You can avoid disputes about spinning again by creating a few "draw cards." Copy the reproducibles from page 94 onto card stock.
2. Laminate the full-page copy, and cut the cards apart.
3. When the spinner lands "on the line," have the player draw one of these cards and then move accordingly.

To Play

1. Assign one student to be the "player" and another student to be the "director."
2. Have the director place the point of a pencil through a paper clip in the center of the plate, and then spin the paper clip.
3. Ask the player to start at the top left corner of the shower curtain and to move the number of spaces indicated by where the paper clip lands. When he gets to the designated spot, he is to read the card he's landed on and answer the question or perform the task described on the card. If he can't answer the question, he goes back to where he was.
4. Tell the player that when he reaches the end of the first row, he should go to the next row and follow that row from right to left. With successive spins of the spinner, he continues zigzagging his way across the shower curtain until he reaches the end.
5. The player's turn ends when he reaches the last square. The director doesn't need to spin the exact number.
6. "Player" and "director" then exchange places and play again.

VARIATIONS

For younger students:

◆ Put on each playing card a picture of a word that begins with a sound you've been working on. When a child lands on that card, he is to name the picture and then say the letter the word begins with. (He might land on the picture, announce that it's a monkey, and say that it begins with "m.")

◆ After the child identifies the picture on the playing card she lands on, have her give a word that rhymes with what's pictured.

◆ If you are exploring with young children the body coverings of different animals, make each playing card show a picture of a snake, bird, bear, or other animal. Divide the spinner plate into four sections: "feathers," "scales," "fur," and "spin again." Include a picture clue with each of these words. Place the cards in the pockets. If the spinner lands on "feathers," the player moves to the next space that shows an animal with that body covering. The challenge is simply to figure out which square the child should be moving to; he doesn't have to do anything more once he gets there.

◆ Divide the plate in fourths and label the sections "air," "sea," "land," and "spin again." Again, use pictures of animals as the playing cards. In this case, if the spinner lands on "sea," for example, the student would move to the next space that shows a sea creature.

Move back
one space

Spin again

Lose a turn

Move ahead
one space

Go back to
the beginning

Move ahead
two spaces

"I Have/Who Has?"

Some people call this "Zip Around" because the answer always ends up back where the game began—with the first plate! Whatever you call it, inexpensive paper plates are the ideal way to "serve up" review and practice in those five minutes before lunch or dismissal.

Getting Ready

1. Start by writing with a red permanent marker an "I have___" statement (e.g., "I have A") at the top of the first plate.

2. Under that statement, with a blue permanent marker, write, "Who has_____?" (For example, "Who has B?")

3. At the top of the next plate, write in red the answer to the question on the first plate ("I have B.").

4. Underneath that, write a new question in blue ("Who has C?").

5. Continue writing answers and questions on plates until you get to the last plate. That last question will be answered on the first plate.

6. Laminate all the plates so that you can play this game again and again.

MATERIALS
• 10 to 30 lightweight paper plates (9")

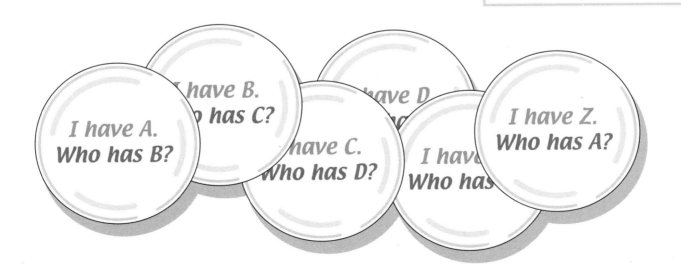

To Play

1. Pass out the plates to the children in your room.
2. If you're working with sequential material (e.g., the ABCs or a story sequence), ask the child who has the first plate in the sequence to go first. Otherwise, ask any child to start the game by standing and reading what's on his plate.
3. As soon as the first child reads his plate, he sits down.
4. The person who has the answer to the first child's question stands and reads her plate.
5. Continue until all of the plates have been read.

TEACHER TIPS

◆ When you're creating the plates, it's helpful to lay them on the floor. Make sure that the question on the last plate ("Who has?") is answered on the first plate ("I have").

◆ When working with young children, introduce this activity by having the students come up to the front of the room and line up in order as they read their plates. Once they understand how the process works, let them stay at their seats.

◆ The consistency of the color coding helps the young learner. Picture clues on the plates help,

too. These students may "read" only the pictures and not the words. But they learn to say the words and to associate those words with the pictures.

◆ If you have more children than plates, children can share the reading. More plates than children? Allow some children to have more than one plate.

◆ To speed the action, time the children as they play, and then ask them if they can "beat the clock." They usually cheer and want to do it again. In that case, have them switch plates and start all over!

Potential "I Have / Who Has" Topics

PHONICS
Plate 1: I have A for apple (picture of apple).
Who has B for bunny? (picture of bunny)
Plate 2: I have B for bunny (picture of bunny).
Who has C for castle? (picture of castle)

NUMBERS
Plate 1: I have 2 + 2.
Who has the number after 6?
Plate 2: I have 7.
Who has the number between 8 and 10?

TIME
Plate 1: I have 3:00.
Who has the hour hand on 4 and the minute hand on 6?
Plate 2: I have 4:30.
Who has both hands pointed to the 12?

GEOGRAPHY
Plate 1: I have the Nile. (This is the answer to "the world's longest river," which goes on the bottom of the final plate.)
Who has the world's tallest mountain?
Plate 2: I have Mt. Everest.
Who has the world's largest island? (The answer would be "Greenland," so "Greenland" goes on the top of Plate 3.)

SCIENCE
Plate 1: I have six legs. (This is the answer to the question on the final plate, "Who has the number of legs on an insect?")
Who has the number of legs on a snake?
Plate 2: I have none.
Who has an animal with a pouch? (This leads to the answer on the next plate: "I have kangaroo.")

STORY SEQUENCE
(For younger students, add a lot of picture support on the plates.)
Plate 1: I have Goldilocks.
Who was the owner of the bowl that was big?
Plate 2: I have Papa Bear.
Who has the owner of the bowl that was small? (Baby Bear)

SPELLING
Plate 1: I have T-H-E-Y.
Who has girl?
Plate 2: I have G-I-R-L.
Who has because?

BUDDY READING AND MORE
Overview

We all tend to remember better what we've read if we have a chance to talk about it with someone else. That's the idea behind buddy reading: Children read together (in pairs), discuss together what they've read, and together complete a task related to the reading.

Buddy reading is a powerful tool in the classroom. Once you've modeled it and guided students in the process while providing feedback, you'll find that pairs of students can listen and discuss pieces of literature at a level that a child reading on his own would be hard pressed to attain.

Talk Spot Cards

PURPOSE
To allow student choice and eliminate confusion

INTELLIGENCES
On-the-move learner
With-friends learner
Word learner

LEARNING STYLES
Auditory learner
Tactile/kinesthetic learner
Visual learner

GROUP SIZE
Pair or triad

SKILLS
Categorizing
Comparing/contrasting
Creative expression
Evaluating
Fix-up strategies
Following directions
Imaging
Inferring
Organization
Predicting/confirming
Problem-solving
Questioning
Sequencing
Synthesizing

AGE GROUP
All ages

Once you've assisted students in finding partners who will work well with them and have read the same book, the next step is to identify a specific place where each pair will meet. Here's a quick and easy way to do that.

Getting Ready

1. Copy the reproducibles on page 100 onto card stock.
2. Laminate the pages and cut them into separate pieces.

Using the Cards

1. Have each pair of students choose a card to reserve their "Talk Spot" for the week.
2. Write both partners' names on a sticky note attached to the card, and display these cards in your room. You can always add other "Talk Spots" that fit your classroom layout and furnishings.
3. At the beginning of the next week, have each pair of students choose a new "Talk Spot" card. Note that talk spots change every week, but partners may stay together for as long as three to four weeks.

MATERIALS
• Sticky notes (3" x 3")

Talk Spots

In the class library

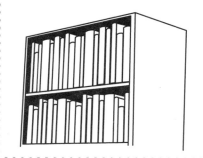

By the window

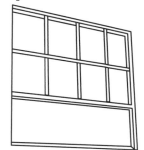

Under the clock

Under the back table

On the beanbag chairs

In the class meeting area

Near the teacher's desk

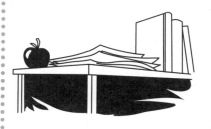

In the science area

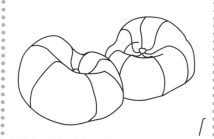

Near the door

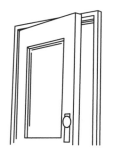

In the writing area

By the book shelf

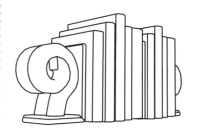

At my desk

Buddy Reading for Younger Pairs

PURPOSE
To encourage rereading for fluency and enhanced comprehension

INTELLIGENCES
On-the-move learner
With-friends learner
Word learner

LEARNING STYLES
Auditory learner
Tactile/kinesthetic learner
Visual learner

GROUP SIZE
Pair or triad

SKILLS
Comparing/contrasting
Evaluating
Fix-up strategies
Following directions
Predicting/confirming
Problem-solving
Questioning

AGE GROUP
Younger

Buddy reading is a great way to boost reading comprehension in both of the "buddies" as children share their reading experiences.

Introducing Buddy Reading

1. You may need to help students find reading buddies who have just read the same book.
2. Before students begin buddy reading, hold a practice session. Have the children sit in a circle, and then ask two children to come to the center of the circle and demonstrate how to speak quietly during

MATERIALS
- Sentence strips
- Story sticks (see page 102)
- Lunch-size paper bags
- Sticks for puppets
- Adding machine tape
- Popsicle sticks

For emergent buddy readers:

If they're tackling a short chapter book, have students stop at the end of each chapter to summarize what happened in the chapter they just read and predict what will happen in the next chapter. After they finish the book, have the two children in each pair take turns retelling the story. Tell them that looking back through the book at this point is not only acceptable, it's encouraged.

buddy reading. Tell them to use "two-inch" quiet voices, not "one-foot" loud voices. You may want to have all the children act out what loud voices are like and what quiet voices are like.

3. Next, have the children act out what it means to listen to each other and encourage each other. Have two different children come to the center of the circle. Have one child start talking while the other child nods and smiles and says, "That's interesting," or "Tell me more," or "Where did you read that?"

4. Explain to students that they will have special assignments for their buddy reading. Each day, you'll choose one of the ideas in the box on the facing page and write those instructions on sentence strips. (You'll probably need more than one strip for each idea.) Tell students you'll place the sentence strip(s) in the reading center or on the chalkboard and announce that this is the "Buddy Reading" task for the day.

The Process

1. Once students are comfortable with the process, they can try it on their own. Choose a fairly simple set of tasks for the first day, and let reading buddies tackle it together.

2. Monitor the progress of the buddies to be sure they understand both the process and the material.

TEACHER TIP

There is one potential problem with buddy reading: When two young children read together, they're supposed to take turns reading aloud and reading along silently. In practice, it's often hard for the child who's not reading aloud to stay on task and read along in his own book.

One way to address that problem is to take a Popsicle stick and draw a black dot on the end. Instruct the silent reader to hold this "story stick" and use it to follow along in his own book as the other child reads aloud. At the end of the page, the children switch roles—and the stick goes to the new silent reader. (It's a good idea to model the exchange of story sticks before asking the children to start using them.)

This gives both children a "job" and leaves no doubt as to what each child is to do. Also, the tactile reminder of using and handing off the stick helps both partners remember who is reading and who is following along. Lose the stick? Not a problem! The kids can make their own.

Buddy Reading Ideas

IDEA #1

Read one page aloud to your buddy.
The buddy reads along with a story stick.
Take turns reading aloud and using the story stick.
Ask your buddy a question about the book.
Answer a question your buddy asks you.

IDEA #2

Read to your buddy.
Let your buddy echo each sentence.
Take turns being the reader and the echo.

IDEA #3

You and your buddy read each page aloud together.
Be sure to start and stop at the same time.
Watch for (.), (?), (!), (,), and (")—punctuation marks.
Read with expression.

IDEA #4

Read the story together.
Take turns reading aloud and using the story stick.

Add sounds to the story.
(Sounds could be animals, doors, footsteps, etc.)

IDEA #5

Read the story together.
Take turns reading aloud and using the story stick.
Make puppets for the story. (Use paper bags or
    sticks.)
Act out the story, using the puppets.
Add talk that puppets might use.

IDEA #6

Read the story together.
Take turns reading aloud and using the story stick.
Choose four scenes from the story.
Draw the scenes in order on adding machine tape.
Add a Popsicle stick to each end of the tape to
    make a scroll story.
Roll the paper up onto the stick on the right side. As
    you tell the story, unroll the paper from the right
    and roll it onto the stick on the left side.

Buddy Reading for Older Pairs

You can enhance reading comprehension among older students, too, by giving them a chance to discuss with their reading buddies what they've read.

Getting Ready

1. Copy the reproducibles on pages 106–10 onto card stock.
2. Laminate the pages, and then cut them into separate cards.

Introducing the Buddy Reading Cards: Day 1

1. Choose a card that's appropriate for a piece of literature that you have read with the entire class.
2. Explain to the class that, "Today, when you pair-share, this is what you are going to do." Write the instructions from the card onto the chalkboard or a chart.
3. Assign partners and have each pair discuss the question.
4. Have each pair write down their shared response on a piece of paper.
5. Ask the pairs to share their responses with the rest of the class.
6. Note similarities and differences in student responses. Celebrate unusual or distinctive responses.

Introducing the Buddy Reading Cards: Day 2

1. Let each pair choose a different piece of literature, but make sure that every option chosen by one pair is chosen by another pair as well (so that pairs can discuss their responses later in groups of four). Have them read the text together, and then ask them to respond to this new reading by answering the questions on the chalkboard or chart from the previous day.
2. For sharing time, let two pairs get together to share their responses.
3. As you are monitoring their discussions, listen for one or two responses that might be shared with the class as a whole. This introduction to the activity provides a model followed by guided response.

On Successive Days

1. Repeat this process with each of the other cards.
2. After you have had an opportunity to go through all of the questions with your class, explain that each child is free to find a partner who has read the same book. After they have chosen one of the cards, they can then respond to the question together.
3. Ask each student to use the last page of his reading journal to record which cards he has completed.

TEACHER TIP

Note that the Poem Questions require two pairs to read the same poem and compare responses—not just on the second day of introducing the cards but every time they're used. When students choose that option, you'll need to monitor choices up front to be sure that two pairs are reading the same poem at the same time.

Name __Jessica__

Name of Card	Partner	Date completed
What's Important?	Amy	10/15
Summarizing	Amanda	10/16
Opinions Matter	Amy	10/17

Buddy Reading

Help, I'm Stuck!

The goal here is to write about a place in the text where you were unclear about what the author had written.

1. Copy the chart below into your journal.
2. Find the actual quote from the text that seems unclear.
3. Write it in the column under "Quote."
4. In the next column, write the question(s) that you would ask the author about that quote.
5. As you continue to read or think about the text, write how you were able to answer your question(s).
6. If you are unable to answer your question by reading the text, ask a partner to discuss that section with you. If you both still have questions, write them on a sticky note for later discussion with the teacher.

Quote	Question	Answered My Question

What's Important?

With your partner, decide what is important in this story. Answer these questions.

1. What information is necessary for the story?

2. What information is just interesting?

3. Is the author's main purpose to tell a story or to present facts? Or is it a combination?

4. Did the author give an opinion? If so, show an example.

5. Did the author include facts? If so, give an example.

6. Ask your partner to answer a question about this text. Make sure that the answer can be found in the book. If your partner needs to read the text again, help him locate the answer to the question.

7. Ask your partner an opinion question about this text. "What do you think would happen if ...?" "How would things be different if ...?"

Summarizing

1. Make sure that you and your partner each have a copy of the same book, plus some sticky notes.

2. Choose a section of the text to focus on. This can be a chapter, three or four pages, or a paragraph.

3. Find three different points in that selection that are important. Write one word on each sticky note to jog your memory about one of those points. While you're doing this, your partner should be doing the same thing.

4. Using the three words, write a summary of the selection in your journal. Your partner should be doing the same thing independently in a separate journal.

5. Share your summary with your partner. Compare and contrast the three points and the summary in your journal with the three points and summary your partner came up with.

6. Describe in your journal the "who," "what," "when," "where," "why," and "how" of your selection. Meanwhile, your partner should be independently writing his own descriptions in his journal.

7. Compare notes with your partner.

Poem Questions

1. With a partner, read a poem.

2. Write down three questions you have about the poem. Your partner should do the same thing with the same poem.

3. Exchange questions and try to answer your partner's questions.

4. Let your partner try to answer your questions.

5. Together, make up three new questions.

6. Find another pair of students who have read the poem.

7. Share your three new questions about the poem with them and try to answer their three questions.

8. With all four of you working together, come up with one question about the poem to discuss with the whole class. For example, while reading "Stopping by the Woods on a Snowy Evening" by Robert Frost, you would come to the line, "my little horse must think it queer to stop without a farmhouse near." You might ask, "Why is he stopping here? Is there something wrong? Did he hear something? Where is he going?"

Opinions Matter

Read a book with a book buddy. After you finish, write your answers to the following questions in your journal while your buddy does the same thing. Then take turns telling each other your answers and discussing the questions. (Each of you should answer all of the questions. You just need to take turns sharing the answers.)

1. What did you like about the story?

2. What didn't you like about the story?

3. Do you have any questions for the author?

4. Is there anything you're unsure of?

5. Did you notice any patterns?

6. Did you make any connections with things you know?

Stay Connected

While you are reading today, use small sticky notes to mark places where you were unsure of what was happening in the book. This may be:

- a word you are unsure of
- a place where you were confused about what was happening
- a place where you didn't understand why a character was saying or doing something
- an illustration that is confusing

Be ready to share your notes and questions with a partner.

Share Your Finds

Today, while you are reading, be looking for interesting phrases or descriptive words that the author uses to give you a strong mental picture of what is happening in the story. Ask yourself, "How did the author do that to me?"

1. Mark each of those passages with a sticky note.

2. Be ready to share those words or phrases with a partner.

3. With your partner, decide on two or three words or phrases that you might like to use in your own writing. Add these to your journal or put them on a large piece of construction paper, and then decorate that paper and share what you've found with the class.

Exploring Nonfiction

8

Read your nonfiction book with a scientific approach. Scientists are always asking questions. Here's a way you and a partner can be like them.

1. Choose a selection out of your book. This could be a page or a part of a chapter.
2. Lay your hand on a portion of the selection. This could be a page or a paragraph.
3. Lift your hand and read to yourself the section that your hand had covered.
4. Stop, re-cover the text with your hand, and tell your partner what you have read.
5. Decide what you both think the author will tell you about next.
6. Switch roles. Let your partner read the next "handful" of text, and then stop and retell that part to you. Together, think about what questions you might have for the next "handful" of text.
7. Continue this process until you reach the end of the selection.
8. At the end of your selected text, write or draw the main ideas contained in what you have just read.
9. Decide where to look for the answers to any unanswered questions. Could you go to a class "expert," a school expert, another book, a parent expert, the Internet, the newspaper, or a magazine? What other sources could you use?

Passing Notes

9

1. Choose a partner who has read the same book. The rest of these instructions are for both of you.
2. Use a sticky note to mark a part of your book that you want to talk to your partner about. This can be a sentence or two. It can be something that made you *stop and reread,* something that was *confusing,* or *something that happened to you, too!*
3. Write this "memorable quote" on an index card. Exchange quotes with your partner.
4. While your partner does the same thing, take a piece of white 8½" x 11" paper and fold it into four equal sections, like a greeting card. Unfold the paper and number the sections 1 through 4.
5. Together, choose one of the two quotes.
6. Write that quote in section 1 of your paper while your partner does the same thing on his paper.
7. In section 2, write your personal thoughts and feelings about this quote, as well as your reactions to it. Your partner should do the same thing on his paper.
8. Exchange papers. Read what your partner has written. In section 3, write your response to what your partner wrote in section 2.
9. Exchange papers again. Read your partner's response. In section 4, write your response to what your partner wrote in section 3.
10. Discuss the quote with your partner. Talk about the similarities and differences in your responses to the same quote. Then turn the paper over, and repeat the process for the other quote.

Popcorn Grouping

Popcorn Grouping is a simple way to create guided reading groups based on ability or interest level. By creating a listing that "pops" back and forth between your higher-level students and your lower-level students, you can help ensure that your groups will be evenly distributed.

1. Number down your paper until you reach the number of students in your class. If you have 25 students, number from 1 to 25.

2. List your top student on line number 1.

3. List your most struggling student on the last line (i.e., 25th of 25 slots).

4. List your next-to-the-top student on line 2.

5. List your next-to-the-most-struggling student on line 24.

6. Continue going back and forth until you reach that middle group of students that seem to be at the same level.

7. Rank this middle group of students as accurately as possible. If you are in a quandary as to where to place a student, consider two students who are similar to each other and to this child, and ask yourself, "Which student is this child most like?" List the unplaced child in the slot under the student she is most like.

8. Look at your list and see how your students are grouped—which ones are high, which are low, and which are in the middle. Then break the class into groups of similar abilities. Guided reading groups ideally include four to six students. So, if you have a group of eight students who are close in ability, it's better to create two groups of four students each than to group them as a block of eight students.

9. Repeat this Popcorn Grouping process about once a month. Repeating the process keeps you constantly evaluating your students, and prevents students from becoming locked into one group.

Note that Popcorn Grouping isn't always based on skill level. It can also be based on prior knowledge of the subject, interest in the subject, or any other approach to grouping that seems appropriate for the topic. When you group by prior knowledge, for instance, your "experts" can read and contribute in areas of their personal expertise.

Bloom's Reading Task Cards

PURPOSE
To promote higher-level thinking skills

INTELLIGENCES
Construction learner
Nature learner
Number learner
On-my-own learner
On-the-move learner
Rhythmic learner
With-friends learner
Word learner

LEARNING STYLES
Auditory learner
Tactile/kinesthetic learner
Visual learner

GROUP SIZE
Pair or triad
Individual

SKILLS
Categorizing
Comparing/contrasting
Creative expression
Evaluating
Fix-up strategies
Following directions
Imaging
Inferring
Organization
Predicting/confirming
Problem-solving
Questioning
Sequencing
Synthesizing

AGE GROUP
Older

In 1956, Benjamin Bloom developed a classification of the levels of thinking that are part of the learning process. He found that by far the majority of the questions teachers ask fall into the "knowledge" category—the lowest level on Bloom's taxonomy and the one that emphasizes information recall. We have an opportunity to help our students move from simply recalling information to developing much more complex thinking skills. We can do that simply by asking questions that belong in higher levels of the taxonomy and require more "brainpower." These "Bloom's Cards" ask just those kinds of questions.

To Prepare the Cards

1. Copy each page of reproducibles (pages 114–19) onto colored card stock. Use one color for knowledge questions, a different color for comprehension, and so on.
2. Laminate each sheet, and then cut it into separate cards.
3. Punch a hole in the corner of each, and secure the cards of each color with a book ring. This gives you six sets of cards. Each set is a different color, but every set contains five cards and a cover.

To Use the Cards

1. Pair off the children, or instruct them to work independently.
2. Instruct each student or pair to choose a task card and to complete the task on that card. (You may need to guide some students to appropriate choices.)

Basic Bloom's

When you're planning your own questions or asking for student responses, it's helpful to keep Bloom's categories in mind. Here's a quick reference list.

Knowledge: the rote recall of information
Words to use: define, label, recall, select, list, quote, name

Comprehension: reworking the material to create better understanding
Words to use: summarize, explain, describe, in your own words

Application: using information in a new situation
Words to use: apply, practice, illustrate, change, classify

Analysis: looking for relationships within the concept
Words to use: compare, contrast, analyze, give evidence

Synthesis: uniting ideas to make a new whole
Words to use: design, imagine, pretend, rewrite

Evaluation: using certain criteria to judge material
Words to use: assess, judge, rate, rank, appraise, defend

As you rework your questions, remember that the goal is always to develop more complex thinking, not simply to make the task more difficult.

Knowledge

Knowledge #1

Memorize a part of the story you especially liked, and present what you've memorized to the class.

Knowledge #2

1. Choose some of your favorite words from the story.
2. Make a word card for each word on a separate index card.
3. Share the word cards with your partner.

Knowledge #3

Choose one of the following:
1. Make a list of rhyming words from the story.
2. Make a list of "-ing" words from the story.
3. In the story, find words that have prefixes. Make a list of those words.
4. In the story, find words that have suffixes. Make a list of those words.

Knowledge #4

Draw a picture that shows when and where the story takes place.

Knowledge #5

Make a list of the main characters in the story. Next to each character's name, write something about that character.

Comprehension

Comprehension #1

Write a brief summary of the main events in the story.

Comprehension #2

Paint a setting from the story, and then add to that same picture by painting in one of the main characters.

Comprehension #3

Pretend that this book is a movie coming to your town. Tape-record an ad for the movie.

Comprehension #4

Restate the main problem in the story. What was the cause of the problem?

Comprehension #5

Make a picture dictionary of new words from the story.

Application

Application #1

Write or act out another story using the same characters.

Application #2

Pretend that this story is being made into a video. Design a cover for the video case.

Application #3

Make a model of the setting where the story takes place.

Application #4

Make a puppet for each of the characters, and act out the story using the puppets.

Application #5

Do a Reader's Theater using dialogue from the story. Share it with the class.

Analysis

Analysis #1

Make a map showing the places the main character traveled. Include a legend. (The legend might represent railroad crossings, roads, mountains, or streams, for example.)

Analysis #2

Draw a cartoon that shows one of the characters.

Analysis #3

Plan a menu for a meal the main character might eat. Draw the meal and write a description of its contents. Explain why this character would eat this.

Analysis #4

Write a report or make an anchor chart about a specific animal from the story. Explain whether it would make a good pet. Why or why not?

Analysis #5

Make a model of a specific animal from the story.

Synthesis

Synthesis #1

Pretend you are a character from the story. Use suitable facial expressions, body language, and gestures, and have the class guess who you are.

Synthesis #2

Design a costume that one of the characters might have worn. You can draw it or actually create it.

Synthesis #3

Design a bookmark that promotes the book.

Synthesis #4

Plan a vacation that you think the main character would enjoy. Tell the class why it's suitable.

Synthesis #5

Make a "Lost and Found" poster for someone or something from the story.

Evaluation

Evaluation #1

Would you like to read
another book by this author?
Explain why or why not.

Evaluation #2

Would you like to be like or
unlike the main character?
Explain your reasons.

Evaluation #3

Choose a character from the story
who you think would make a good
friend. Explain your choice.

Evaluation #4

Write a letter to the author
asking about the story and telling
why you did or didn't like it.

Evaluation #5

If you could go to the place in which
the story occurred, would you?
Explain why or why not.

Musical Options

The body stores music (and raps, rhymes, and other poetry) in the part of the brain that handles automatic responses—the same part that stores flash cards. What's more fun—music or flash cards? Not a contest! It's definitely music!

The Theory

Music has many advantages. It's a community builder, an activator for language, and a memory enhancer. It can also be a creative outlet for synthesizing and adapting knowledge. Similarly, poetry builds imaging skills that enrich the learning experience, increase comprehension, and support creative writing.

For the struggling reader or second-language learner, seeing and singing the words of a song can imprint language faster than any other reading method. Adding rhythm and beat to words involves the bodily movement that engages the "on-the-move" learner. And for everyone (including the teacher), music and poetry offer a great change of pace in the classroom.

The Practice

The task cards that follow suggest ideas for engaging your students in rhythmical opportunities as well as for actually creating music. All of these tasks can be undertaken in the classroom or completed at home and brought to school. Either way, be sure to provide opportunities for students to share their creations—and encourage everybody to sing and move along.

To prepare these task cards for student use, copy the reproducibles on pages 121–29 onto card stock. Laminate the reproduced pages for durability, and then cut the cards apart. Hand them out as student assignments or let the kids choose their tasks.

Musical Options Task Cards

1. Character Songs

(Write and sing to the tune: "Are You Sleeping?")

Write a song about a character in a book you're reading. Fill in the blanks to create your song, following the sample (based on *The Little Engine That Could*).

_____   _____
who   who

_____   _____
where   where

_____
event

_____
event

_____   _____
end   end

SAMPLE:
Little engine, little engine

On the tracks, on the tracks

Trying to go up the hill,

Thinking positively will

Get him over, get him over!

2. Story Comprehension

Write and sing your own song to the tune, "Are You Sleeping?" Look over the sample based on *Charlotte's Web*, and then fill in the blanks to create your song about a book you're reading.

_____ _____ (spinning, spinning)
adjective   adjective

_____ _____ (caring, loving)
adjective   adjective

_____ (in the barn)
prepositional phrase telling where the character was

_____ (with Wilbert)
prepositional phrase telling where the character was

_____ and _____ (spinning and spelling)
"ing" verb   "ing" verb

_____ and _____ (spinning and spelling)
"ing" verb   "ing" verb

_____ (save the pig)
three-syllable word or phrase to end the story

_____ (the special friend)
another short word or phrase to end the story

---

3. Musical Picture Book

Draw or take a picture of a favorite classroom activity.

Copy the words below onto another sheet of paper. Fill in the blanks with a description of what is happening in the picture. If you want, add another photo for another activity, and describe it by copying these words and filling in the blanks again. Then put all the photos and descriptions together to make a book.

Sing to "The More We Get Together"   **EXAMPLE:**

The more we _____ together, together, together,   (read)

The more we _____ together, the happier are we.   (read)

For my _____ are your _____ and   (books, books)

your _____ are my _____   (books, books)

The more we _____ together, the happier are we.   (read)

4. Spelling Songs

Sing your spelling words to the following tunes:

For four-letter words: "Ten Little Indians"

"C-o-m-e, come is my word,
C-o-m-e, come is my word,
C-o-m-e, come is my word,
I can spell this word."

For five-letter words: "Row, Row, Row Your Boat"

"H-o-u-s-e, house is my word.
H-o-u-s-e, house is my word."

5. More Spelling Songs

Sing your spelling words to the following tunes:

For six-letter words: "Happy Birthday"

"L-i-t-t-l-e
L-i-t-t-l-e
L-i-t-t-l-e
Little is my word."

For seven-letter words: "Twinkle, Twinkle, Little Star"

"B-e-c-a-u-s-e
B-e-c-a-u-s-e
B-e-c-a-u-s-e
B-e-c-a-u-s-e
B-e-c-a-u-s-e
Because is my word."

6. Play a Word

Start with a portable keyboard and individual sticky letters. Attach the letters "a" to "z" in order to the keys. Play and sing the letters of your spelling words or vocabulary words.

---

7. Old MacWho?

Write a new version of "Old MacDonald," using a character from a book you're reading. Try it first with the story of Pinocchio.

Old _____ had a _____,   (Giupetto, store)

_____.   (making children toys)

And (in) (on) that _____ he had   (store)

Some _____.   (tools)

Repeat line 2 _____   (making children toys)

With a _____ here and a _____ there   (tap-tap, tap-tap)

Here a _____, there a _____, everywhere a _____- _____,   (tap, tap, tap-tap)

Old _____ had a _____,   (Giupetto, store)

_____.   (making children toys)

8. Geography Sing-a-Long

Use the tune "Shortnin' Bread" and fill in the special things of your town or city.

I live in _____ (city), _____ (city), _____ (city).   (Houston)

I live in _____ (city). It's my home.   (Houston)

With _____ _____, _____ _____   (busy highways, tall skyscrapers)

I live in _____ (city). It's my home.   (Houston)

It's where I work and where I play. It's the place I want to stay.

I live in _____ (state), _____ (state), _____ (state).   (Texas)

I live in _____ (state). It's my home.   (Texas)

With _____ (state bird) and _____ (state flower)   (mockingbirds, bluebonnets)

I live in _____ (state). It's my home.   (Texas)

It's where I work and where I play. It's the place I want to stay.

---

9. Mother Goose on the Loose

Make up your own version of a Mother Goose rhyme. Here's an example.

> To market, to market to buy a fat bull,
> Home again, home again, jiggety-jewel!
>
> To market, to market to buy a fat turkey,
> Home again, home again, jiggety-jerky!

Illustrate your Mother Goose rhyme and be ready to share your rhythmic version with the class.

10. Listen and Paint

Listen to the words of a favorite song. As you think about the words, what pictures do you see in your mind? Use watercolors to paint the images and colors the song creates in your mind. Share your pictures and music with someone.

If you make several pictures, use them to create a book. On each page, write the words from the song that go with the picture on that page. Now someone else can listen to your "songbook" with the music playing.

To get yourself started, try "It's a Wonderful World" by Louis Armstrong.

11. Poetry and Music

Choose a favorite poem and match it with a song you think fits the mood or the words of the poem. Copy the poem onto an overhead transparency or onto a chart. Play the music while you read the poem aloud to the class and show your transparency or chart.

12. Play Your Own Tune

Create your own musical bottles from empty glass bottles with lids. (YooHoo bottles work very well.) Pour water into 10 bottles, making the water come to a different level in each bottle. That gives you 10 notes (the eight notes of the scale plus one lower and one higher). If you use food coloring to make the water in each bottle a different color, it makes the different tones more memorable. Number the bottles from 0 to 10. Use a spoon to lightly tap the bottles and play the numbers in your telephone number.

Write down, in order, the colors of the bottles of water that make up your telephone tune.

Now write about the feeling your tune suggests. Does it sound sad? Happy? Eerie?

13. Graph Your Telephone Number

It's fun to graph your phone number. Use 1" graph paper. Going from left to right across the graph, write each number of your telephone number across the bottom. Place one number under each vertical line of the graph paper. Above each number in your telephone number, make a dot on the graph paper. (If the first number in your telephone number were 7, you would put a dot on the graph paper 7 blocks from the bottom.) When you are through graphing your number, connect the dots to see how your telephone number moves up and down. To make the path even more dramatic, paint different colors along the path of your graph until you fill your paper.

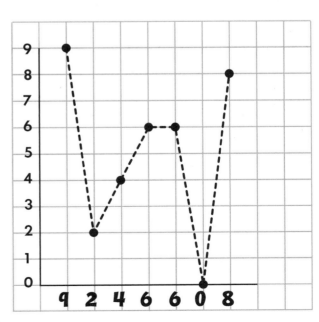

14. Sound Stories

Start with a story, a tape recorder, and a blank tape. Choose a story to read into the tape recorder. Add background noises (doors opening and closing, footsteps, knocks on the door, and so on) to illustrate the sounds you might hear if the story were a "live" production. Share your sound story with a friend or the class.

15. Song Picture Books

Choose one of the following sequence songs and create a picture for each line of the song. Using a tape recorder and a blank tape, record the song to go with your pictures. Feel free to change the story or add extra scenes.

"There's a Hole in the Bottom of the Sea"   "Aiken Drum"

"There's a Hole in the Bucket"   "The Farmer in the Dell"

"She'll Be Coming 'Round the Mountain"   "The Hokey Pokey"

"There Was an Old Lady Who Swallowed a Fly"   "Down by the Bay"

"Twelve Days of Christmas"   "Old MacDonald"

"The Wheels on the Bus"   "Skip to My Lou"

"This Is the Way (We Wash Our Clothes ...)"

16. Write a List Poem

Think of a subject.

Make a list of words that describe that subject.

Think of how your subject looks, feels, tastes, and smells, and what sounds it might make.

Your list can range from one to three or more words.

Make a poem using some of the words from your list.

You might write, for example, something like this.

Hamburgers are:
meaty
ketchup-y
juicy
cheesy
delicious
My favorite food!

17. A Rap and a Ho, Ho, Ho

Using a rhythmic rap, write a summary of a book you have read. Include some of the interesting features that will help "sell" your book to the rest of the class. Create a cover for your upcoming CD that will feature the rap from this book. Be ready to share your rap with the class. Feel free to ask one or two of your classmates to join you for the performance.

THE READING RESPONSE FOLDER
Overview

Each of your students will need a place to keep a record of her independent work. Here's one way to set up a simple but useful Reading Response Folder to keep all of a child's reading records in one place.

Before class, put together a three-pronged, two-pocket folder for each student. For each younger student, label the left pocket "Center Work" and the right pocket "Independent Reading"; then place a Choice Card wallet in the left pocket and a Tic-Tac-Go Menu in the right pocket. For each older student, place a Choice Card wallet and CHOMP menu in one pocket and a Weekly Reading Log in the other pocket. (Adjust these choices, of course, as necessary for the age of your students and the needs of your class.)

In the prongs of each folder, place a hole-punched copy of whichever of the reproducibles on pages 131–34 and page 151 are appropriate for your class.

In addition to the folder, students will need some supplies for recording their reading log responses. Assuming that these supplies will need to come from home, I've found that it's helpful to send home a note that explains the concept of the Reading Response Folder and lists the supplies the student will need: a highlighter, a fine-point pen, a small spiral notebook, 3-inch and 3x5-inch sticky notes, 3x5 index cards, colored paper clips, and a resealable quart-size plastic bag to hold all these things.

TEACHER TIPS

◆ When you're reproducing the pages to go in the prongs of the folders, copy each master onto paper of a different color. This helps children know which page to turn to.

◆ For the Daily School Reading Log, types of reading materials will vary depending on what is available in your classroom. You may want to adjust the lists at the bottom of this reproducible accordingly.

Choosing a Good Book for You

(for Younger Students)

1. Read the title. Look at the picture on the cover. Does it look interesting?

2. Read the back cover. Does the book sound like something you would like to read?

3. Read the first three pages. Are there more than three words you don't know?

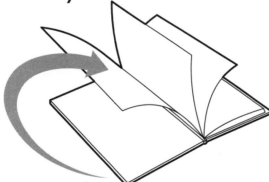

4. Ask your friends if they have read this book. Did they enjoy reading this book or another book by the same author?

5. Look through the book. Do the pictures and print make you think that you would enjoy reading it?

**Did your book pass these tests?
Then this is a good book for you!**

Choosing a Good Book for You
(for Older Students)

1. Read the summary on the back of the book. Does it sound interesting?

2. Page through the chapters and read the titles, or read the table of contents. Do the chapter titles sound interesting to you?

3. Ask your friends if they have read this book or other books by this author. Did they enjoy reading this book or author?

4. Read the information about the author. Does the author sound interesting?

5. Look through the book. Do the photographs, artwork, and print make you think that you would enjoy reading this book?

6. Read the first page. Put one finger down for each word you don't know. (This is the five-finger test.) If you put down all five fingers, the book may be too hard for you. Do you still want to read more?

7. Read the first few chapters. Talk to someone about what you are noticing the author is telling you. Do you want to read on and find out more?

Did your book pass these tests? Then this is a good book for you!

Daily School Reading Log

Name _____ Date _____

	Title:	Author:	Type of reading material:
1			
2			
3			
4			
5			
6			
7			
8			
9			

TYPES OF READING MATERIAL

For younger students:

Magazines	ABC books	Math books
Nonfiction	Poetry	Fairy tales
Big books	Animal fiction	

For older students:

Magazines	Biography	Math books
Nonfiction	Short Story Collection	Poetry
Drama	Realistic fiction	Historical fiction

Daily Home Reading Log

(for Younger Students)

Name _____ Date _____

Title:	Parent signature/date:	Comments:
1		
2		
3		
4		
5		
6		
7		
8		
9		

DIRECTIONS FOR PARENTS:

◆ Your student should be bringing a book home from school every day to read at home that night. In first grade, a child is usually expected to read for 10 minutes each night in order to complete the book in an evening. A rule of thumb is that a child is asked to read an additional 5 to 10 minutes each night as he progresses to each of the next grades.

◆ Additional reading from other books, magazines, and newspapers is also encouraged, although it doesn't need to be included in this log.

◆ Listen to your student read each night. In the first column, fill in (or have your child fill in) the name of the material being read. In the next column, add your signature on the same line, showing that the child did complete the reading. Please feel free to add any comments about your student's reading (fluency, difficulty, book choices, etc.) in the third column. Then please send this sheet back to school with the reading material the next morning.

Weekly Reading Log
(FOR OLDER STUDENTS)

The best way to build reading stamina is to practice, practice, practice. This log tracks the student's reading both at school and at home.

The Process

1. Make one copy of the reproducible on page 136 for each child in the class.

2. Hand out a copy to each student, as well as an explanatory note to go home to that child's parents.

3. Explain to students that each child is expected to devote a certain amount of time each day to reading, and to record in the log both the time he spends and the number of pages he reads.

4. Also explain that each day's reading time includes the reading done at home. Tell the students that at the end of each week, you will sign in the "Teacher signature" block. This shows that you agree that the child has completed what he says he's completed at school. The child's parent needs to sign off that the student has done what he says he's done at home.

5. Tell the students that they're expected to read at home on the weekend, too, though their weekend reading material may involve more magazines and newspapers rather than books. On the weekend, they should note what they read and how much time they spend reading it.

6. Finally, explain that at the end of the two weeks, each student should evaluate his own progress at the bottom of the form. Use these comments as a basis for your teacher-student conferences.

7. At the end of the two weeks, replace the completed logs with a fresh one for each student.

8. Place the completed logs in your individual student files so you can keep track of student progress. These logs are also good references for highlighting progress during parent-teacher conferences.

Weekly Reading Log

Student _____ Beginning Date _____

WEEK 1:

	MONDAY	TUESDAY	WEDNESDAY	THURSDAY	FRIDAY	WEEK TOTAL	SIGN-OFFS
School time: Number of pages:							Teacher signature:
Home time: Number of pages:							Parent signature:

Weekend Journal:

Total time read: Saturday: _____ Sunday: _____

What I read: _____

WEEK 2:

	MONDAY	TUESDAY	WEDNESDAY	THURSDAY	FRIDAY	WEEK TOTAL	SIGN-OFFS
School time: Number of pages:							Teacher signature:
Home time: Number of pages:							Parent signature:

Weekend Journal:

Total time read: Saturday: _____ Sunday: _____

What I read: _____

Personal evaluation of progress these two weeks:

_____

_____

_____

Task Cards for Reading Log Responses

As your students read fiction and nonfiction books, use the reproducible task cards to provide a structure for the responses in the students' reading logs.

Getting Ready

1. Copy the task cards onto card stock. Laminate the copies. Cut the sheets apart into individual cards.
2. You may want to punch a hole in the corner of each card and use a book ring to keep each group of cards together.

Using the Cards

1. As he works with the task cards, ask each student to record his responses on a page to be stored in his Reading Response Folder.
2. Encourage students to work with a variety of task cards and to strive for creativity in their responses.
3. As they gain confidence, urge students to create their own variations on these cards. Watch them take ownership of the process.

TEACHER TIPS

- As students work with these task cards, you'll need a way to track which cards each child has used. One approach is to reserve a page at the front or back of each child's response folder to record this information.
- Note that not all the cards should be used with every selection or with every child. You will want to guide each child to the cards that are most appropriate for the book she is reading and the skills she has demonstrated.
- The shorter task cards, each with simple instructions and a single task, are designed for struggling students and those who are overwhelmed when they face many choices. With the other cards, you might ask some students to complete all the choices on a card and direct other children to selected tasks. This card assignment will depend on the maturity of the individual students and their abilities to deal with multiple tasks.

FICTION

FICTION #1

Main Idea (Comprehension)

1. What is this story about?

2. The best title for this story would be

_____.

3. Choose two words to describe the story. Tell about the story in one sentence using those two words.

4. Write a headline that would be appropriate for this story if it were printed in the newspaper.

FICTION #2

Relationships (Comprehension)

1. Pick two characters in the story. How did they get along? How were they alike? How were they different?

2. _____ is like _____
   (character)   (animal)

   because _____.

3. _____ is like _____
   (character)   (color)

   because _____.

4. _____ is like _____
   (character)   (emotion)

   because _____.

FICTION #3

Drawing Conclusions (Comprehension)

1. What clues in the story made you think the story would end the way it did?

2. Did you think that what the author wrote was a good way to end the story? Why or why not?

3. If you were to write the ending differently, what would you change?

4. How would you continue this story?

Characters (Reader Response)

1. Who were the main characters?

2. Was there one character that you liked? Who? Why?

3. Was there one character that you disliked? Who? Why?

4. Choose a character from the story. Why was this character important to the story?

5. Did any of the characters do things that you thought were wrong? What should they have done?

6. Draw a picture of one of the characters.

Setting (Reader Response)

1. Where did the story take place?

2. Have you ever been to a place like this? Where was it? When were you there?

3. Did this story take place a long time ago? Or now? Or in the future? How do you know?

4. Create a "map" of the main location of the story. Include any roads, hills, rivers, oceans, and so on.

FICTION #6

Mood (Reader Response)

1. How did you feel while reading this book? Why?

2. What was the funniest part?

3. What was the saddest part?

4. What was the most exciting part?

5. What do you remember most about the story?

6. If you were to paint a picture about the feeling the story created, what colors would you use and why?

FICTION #7

Author (Reader Response)

1. What was the author trying to tell you?

2. What did the author have to know to write this book?

3. What sorts of things did your author like or dislike? (People? Places? Behavior? Feelings?)

4. Quote some "sensational sentences" from the book to show how the author described some of the things he liked or disliked.

5. Find another book by this author. Find any similarities or differences between the two books. Create a diagram to show your findings.

Style (Reader Response)

1. What special words did the author use to help you "see" things in the story?

2. What special words did the author use to help you "hear" things in the story?

3. What special words did the author use to help you "feel" things in the story?

4. How did you picture the setting?

5. How did you picture the characters?

6. How did you picture the action?

7. Find and list some "fabulous phrases" that the author used to create these mental pictures.

8. Draw a picture of your favorite part of the story. Below the picture, write what is happening.

NONFICTION

NONFICTION #1

Wonderings

1. What would you like to learn from this book?

2. In your book, locate the title, table of contents, glossary, and chapter headings.

3. In how many places can you find the *title* of the book?

4. How many chapters are listed in the *table of contents?* Do you need to read them in the order that they're listed? Or can you read them out of order?

5. List some things from the *glossary* that you would like to know more about.

6. Based on some of the chapter headings, write some questions that you would ask the author.

NONFICTION #2

Captions

1. What do the captions tell you that the text does not?

2. Draw your own version of one of the illustrations and create a caption for your artwork.

3. Take a photo of something from nature—maybe a flower, a leaf, or an animal—or find a photo in a magazine. Write a caption for your picture, explaining what's in the photo to someone who has never seen this thing before. What makes this object unique?

4. Now label the parts of the object. You can use sticky notes for this.

NONFICTION #3

Research

1. Name a topic from your reading that you would like to learn more about.
2. Now think about what resources you could go to for more information on that topic.
3. List all the locations (school library, public library, and so on) you could go to.
4. Next, list all the media sources (newspapers and magazines) you could go to.
5. Now list all the people who might be good sources of information on this topic.
6. Create a web diagram to show all the resources you've thought of.
7. Look in your classroom and in your school library to see what specific books and other materials might help in your research. Ask your parents and friends about the topic. Look on the Internet for more information. Add these resources to your web diagram.
8. Decide which sources might give you the information you will need. In your diagram, circle the names of those sources.

NONFICTION #4

Put on a Show

1. Create a documentary show on your topic. This can be a live show, or you can create an audiotape or videotape.

2. Include as many diagrams and pictures as you can. (Use the computer for this if you want.)

3. Share your show with the class.

Show Your Changes in Thinking

Create a table that shows how your thinking about your topic has changed as a result of reading this book. In one column write, "Before, I thought ...." In the next column, write, "Now, I think ...."

Before, I thought...	Now, I think...

Questions and Answers

1. Before reading a chapter, turn each of that chapter's subheadings into a question.

2. Write down those questions.

3. After you finish reading the chapter, answer your questions.

Make Predictions

1. Before reading a chapter in your book, take a "picture walk" through the chapter. Read the captions and make predictions about the content of the chapter.

2. Based on your predictions, write down three questions that you expect will be answered in this chapter.

3. Read the chapter.

4. Go back to your questions and write down the answers you've learned from your reading.

✄

Paired Reading

1. Find two books about the same subject. One needs to be nonfiction and one, fiction.

2. Look for factual information in the fictional book. How does the author use this information to tell the story?

3. Construct a comparison chart to show the differences in the two books you have chosen. Look for differences in layout, labels, captions, chapter headings, use of photos versus drawings, and any other things you can find that show how the information is used differently in each case.

VOCABULARY

VOCABULARY #1

New Words

1. Before you read the book, list all the individual words you can think of that relate to the topic of this book.

2. Read the book.

3. Create a chart that shows new words from your reading as well as those you wrote down before you started reading. (If you were reading *Chickens*, by Diane Snowball, your list before reading might include "eggs" and "hens." After reading, you might add "incubator" and "wobbly legs.")

Words into Pictures

Create a mental image of your vocabulary word. Draw a picture that shows what this word makes you think of.

Predicting

1. Take five new vocabulary terms and write down what you think each word means.

2. Ask a friend what she thinks each word means.

3. Look up each of your words in the dictionary.

4. Compare your guesses with what you find in the dictionary and/or what your friend thinks the word means.

5. Now make up a sentence for each word.

Root Words, Prefixes, and Suffixes

Look at your new vocabulary terms. Underline root words in one color, prefixes in a second color, and suffixes in a third color.

re•place•ment

Combining

1. Find 10 terms from your nonfiction book.

2. Write each term on a separate sticky note.

3. See if you can combine two or three of these terms in a sentence, and then tell your sentence to a friend.

4. Let your friend try putting the words together in a different combination.

larvae

habitat

transform

Monthly Book Project

PURPOSE
To spread the word about good books and to develop organization and presentation skills

INTELLIGENCES
With-friends learner
Word learner

LEARNING STYLES
Auditory learner
Visual learner

GROUP SIZE
Pair or triad
Individual

SKILLS
Comparing/contrasting
Evaluating
Following directions
Organization

AGE GROUP
All ages

MATERIALS
• Tape recorder
• Blank audiotape

Using read-aloud books, model each of the options listed at the bottom of the reproducible on the facing page. Don't start the Monthly Book Project until you have done this; the children need to know your expectations.

Rationale

The Monthly Book Project covers many bases.
1. It enables students to hear about books they might want to read.
2. It holds students accountable for the independent activity of maintaining their reading logs.
3. It lets students choose ways to share their reading experiences.
4. It addresses standards that require students to have experience speaking in front of their peers. (Oral language development is important at any age.)

The Process

1. Make one copy of the reproducible for each student.
2. Three-hole-punch the copies.
3. Give a copy of the reproducible to each child in the class. Have the child insert it into the prongs of her Reading Response Folder.
4. Say to students, **"Once a month, you will be expected to share one of your books or a collection of books (ones that are by the same author or have the same theme). Think about 'selling' your book(s) to your classmates, so that they will want to read what you have shared with them this month. This is a sign-up sheet for your Monthly Book Project. You can choose to share your book(s) using some of the suggestions at the bottom of this form. If you'd rather share in a different way, check with me first."**
5. Explain that every month, each student should decide which book he wants to read and which project he wants to try, and then fill in the blanks and get your approval.
6. Add that any child may repeat the same choice in a future month, but that it's better to explore as many different ways of sharing book(s) as possible.
7. Tell students that between projects, each child should store his copy of the reproducible in his Reading Response Folder.

Monthly Book Project

Name _____

Project Choice:	Book:	Book Sharing Date:
1		
2		
3		
4		
5		
6		
7		
8		
9		

Project Possibilities:

- Construct a chart showing the main story elements of your book.
- Audio tape a discussion of a book with a friend. Talk about the main ideas in the story. As the two of you discuss what you've read, try to encourage other students to read this book after listening to your tape.
- Give a Book Talk on several books by one author.
- Compare two of your books with a Venn diagram.
- Your choice: _____

_____

Choice Cards and Wallets for Younger Students

PURPOSE
To build independent workers

INTELLIGENCES
Construction learner
Nature learner
Number learner
On-my-own learner
On-the-move learner
Rhythmic learner
With-friends learner
Word learner

LEARNING STYLES
Auditory learner
Tactile/kinesthetic learner
Visual learner

GROUP SIZE
Pair or triad
Individual

SKILLS
Categorizing
Comparing/contrasting
Creative expression
Evaluating
Fix-up strategies
Following directions
Imaging
Inferring
Organization
Predicting/confirming
Problem-solving
Questioning
Sequencing
Synthesizing

AGE GROUP
Younger

Students need options when they are working on their own. Choice Cards provide those options. They give broad assignments ("Read a fairy tale"), allowing the child some choice within each assignment. They also allow the child to determine the order in which he wants to accomplish each task. Each student can then work independently and at his own pace. Choice Cards can be used during free time, after a child finishes other work, or during any other time you designate.

Establish Student Book Collections

Start by making sure that each child has his own classroom book collection. A book collection is a group of books that the student has gathered from the classroom library for his own private reading. This collection can be kept in a gallon-size resealable plastic bag. Every two weeks, the student returns to the classroom library those books he has read, and then selects new ones. Teachers can assist younger children who are having difficulty making choices. An individual child's collection usually contains easy reads, just-right reads from the guided reading lesson, and wish books. Wish books are ones that the child would like to read—and that he can read together with a more capable reader in the classroom or by following along with an audiotape made of the book.

Put the Wallets Together

1. Start with a file folder. Leaving the folder closed, cut it in half through the fold.
2. Take one of the folder halves and lay it down so that the fold is on the left, and the open ends on the right (like a book).

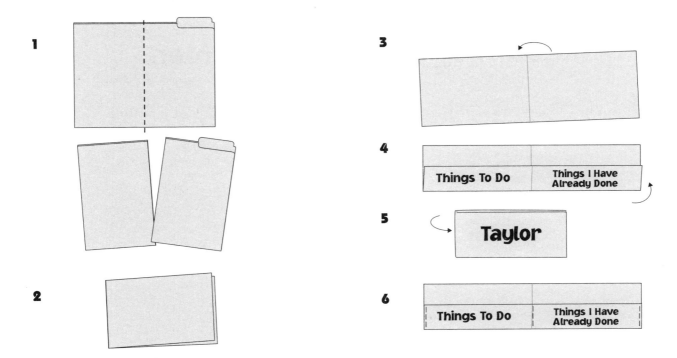

3. Open the folder and lay it flat.

4. Fold up the bottom about two inches. Crease it heavily. Don't staple—yet! On the left flap of the wallet, write "Things To Do." On the right flap, write "Things I Have Already Done."

5. On the front of the wallet, write the child's name.

6. Open up the folder so that it has no folds or creases. Laminate the wallet. Then refold the wallet along the crease lines. Staple the sides and up the middle so that you have two pockets and the wallet can be closed.

7. Repeat with the other half of the file folder.

8. Copy onto lightweight card stock the reproducibles on pages 154–59, as well as any other Choice Cards that you want to add, making one complete set for each child in the class.

9. Laminate the Choice Cards, cut them apart, and insert one set in the left pocket of each wallet.

Begin the Process

1. Present each student in the class with his own wallet of Choice Cards.

2. Explain to the class that as a student completes each task, he should move the card for that task from the left ("Things To Do") to the right ("Things I Have Already Done") pocket of the folder.

3. Add that each child is free to choose the order in which he wants to complete the activities on the cards, but he isn't allowed to repeat any until he has used all of his Choice Cards. When he has completed all of the tasks and has moved all of the cards to the right pocket, he can start over, again choosing the order he prefers.

MATERIALS
- One manila folder for every two children in your class
- Audiotapes of books
- Tape player
- Ziploc bag (1 gallon size)

TEACHER TIP

As you copy the reproducible Choice Cards, don't hesitate to omit any that aren't quite right for your classroom, and add any others that are appropriate for the options available to your students. At the beginning of the year, for example, teachers with young students may want to add activities involving puzzles, art, and building blocks. You may also want to ask your students for suggestions of other choices to add.

Read the room with a pointer. **1**

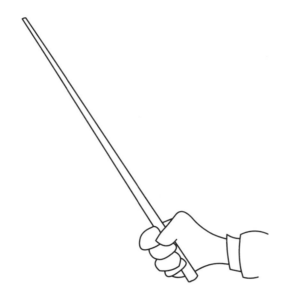

Read a book from your book collection. **2**

Read a big book.

Read a fairy tale.

Read a nonfiction book. 5

Read a class book. 6

Read from your journal.

Read an ABC book.

Write a letter to a friend, your teacher, or someone in your family.

Follow along while you listen to a book in the listening area.

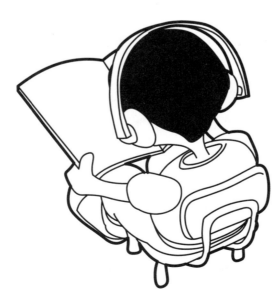

Read from your writing folder.

Read a poem.

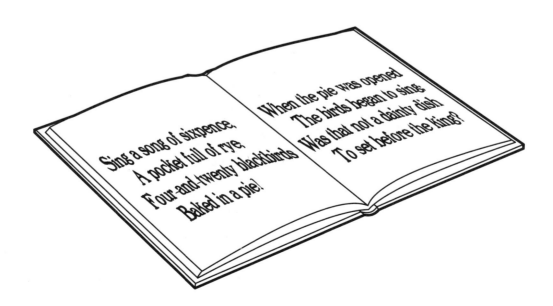

Sing a song of sixpence,
A pocket full of rye,
Four and twenty blackbirds
Baked in a pie.

When the pie was opened
The birds began to sing,
Was that not a dainty dish
To set before the king?

Choice Cards and Wallets for Older Students

Choice Card wallets for older students are constructed differently than those for younger students, but they serve the same purpose. The cards I've chosen to get you started describe tasks that could be completed within one or two literacy periods. If students are asked to share one of their favorite responses once a month, you will find children taking greater pride in their work as well as using evaluation as they choose their best response!

Preparing the Cards and Wallets

1. Copy the reproducibles on pages 162–63.
2. Laminate the copies, and then cut the cards apart.
3. Laminate the library pockets. Use a sharp blade to cut through the lamination at the top of each library pocket, creating a slit so that you can insert a card.
4. Lay the pockets side by side on a table and use wide, clear mailing tape to hold the two pockets together in the middle.
5. Turn the pockets over and tape the backs of the pockets together in the same way.
6. Now you have made a wallet. You will need a set of cards and a wallet for each student.

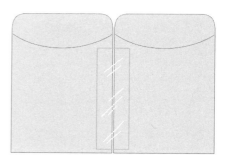

To Use the Choice Cards

1. Place the cards in one side of the wallet.
2. As the student uses a card and completes the task, he moves the card for that task to the other side of the wallet.
3. When all tasks are completed, the student shuffles the cards and begins the process again. (Additional task cards can be designed by the teacher and, with the teacher's approval, by the students.)

Accountability

1. Responses can be written in a journal or on individual sheets of paper.
2. Each response should be shared with the teacher or a fellow student, either in small groups or with the whole class.
3. The student should keep a record (numbered 1 through 12), writing next to each number a note of what she did that day.

TEACHER TIP

Use the Choice Cards with books students are reading on their own, in literacy circles, or in a guided reading lesson.

1

Draw a story map with scenes from your book—in order!

2

Choose two characters from two different books. What might happen if they should meet?

3

Make a graphic organizer for your book. (This can be a Venn diagram, a story map, a character map, or a time line.)

4 Create a KWL chart about a subject or character. Show what you think you know, what you want to know, and (after reading the text) what you learned.

5

Construct a model to show how the main setting might look. Use small boxes and construction paper.

6

Answer these questions about your story: Who? What? Where? When? How?

7 Become a word detective! In your reading materials, find a spelling pattern or rhymes or suffixes or new vocabulary. Make a list on adding machine tape.

8 Redesign the cover of your book. Add your name as the illustrator.

9 Make a puppet to represent the main character. Make up a speech for your character to explain the story.

10 Create a "Wanted" poster for a character in the book.

11 Write a newspaper article about a nonfiction book. Illustrate it with a picture, diagram, cutaway, labels, and/or captions.

12 Connect yourself to the story. Explain how something in your life is like something that happened in the story.

Tic-Tac-Go Menu

PURPOSE
To support student choice within a framework of teacher-directed options

INTELLIGENCES
Construction learner
Nature learner
Number learner
On-my-own learner
On-the-move learner
Rhythmic learner
With-friends learner
Word learner

LEARNING STYLES
Auditory learner
Tactile/kinesthetic learner
Visual learner

GROUP SIZE
Individual

SKILLS
Categorizing
Comparing/contrasting
Creative expression
Evaluating
Fix-up strategies
Following directions
Imaging
Inferring
Organization
Predicting/confirming
Problem-solving
Questioning
Sequencing
Synthesizing

AGE GROUP
Younger

Using a Tic-Tac-Go menu provides students with choices, but it also preserves accountability. The menus can be especially good tools for students who need either extra support or a special challenge.

Getting Ready

1. Make one copy of the reproducible on page 166.
2. In the chart, fill in options that are appropriate for the students who will be using the menu.
3. Repeat the first two steps to create different versions for students with different abilities, intelligences, and/or interests.

The Process

1. Have each child choose a book from her book collection or independent reading.
2. Give the child a copy of the completed Tic-Tac-Go menu that is appropriate for her reading level and interests.
3. Ask the child to select from the choices on the grid four activities that she wants to complete, and to list her choices on the lines at the bottom of the page.

TEACHER TIP

Stumped for sources for puzzles? Go to www.puzzlemaker.com to find lots of great puzzles. Or let the kids explore this site themselves. As early as second grade, children can handle this on their own.

4. Tell her that if she prefers, she can invent an alternative to one of the four choices and list that on the "Special choices" line—but she needs to get your written okay on that one before proceeding.

5. Have her complete the remaining lines at the bottom of the form.

6. Have her complete the chosen activities and share the results with the class.

MATERIALS
- Crossword puzzles
- Connect-the-dot puzzles
- Tape player
- Audiotape of a story

Tic-Tac-Go Menu

1. Draw	**2. Act it out**	**3. Tell**
Draw a story.	Act out the story.	Tell the story in your own way.
4. Puzzle-solve	**5. Rhyme or sing**	**6. Count**
Solve a crossword puzzle or connect-the-dots puzzle with the theme of your story.	Learn a rhyme or song that's appropriate for the story, or make one up for the class.	Survey your class to learn how students feel about the story. Create a graphic organizer to show the results of your survey. Write down or tell the class what your survey showed.
7. Listen	**8. Build**	**9. Change it**
Listen to any taped story. Compare and contrast that story to the one we read in class.	Build a home for one of the characters in your book.	Create a new ending for a story you've read or one we've read in class. Tell the class what you've come up with.

Pick any four choices: #___1___, #___5___, #___8___, and #___9___.

Special choices: _____

Teacher okay: _____

Name(s) ___Whitney_____

Date: ___10/1/04___   Date when due: ___10/8/04___

Tic-Tac-Go Menu

1. Draw	2. Act it out	3. Tell
4. Puzzle-solve	5. Rhyme or sing	6. Count
7. Listen	8. Build	9. Change it

Pick any four choices: #_____, #_____, #_____, and #_____.

Special choices: _____

Teacher okay: _____

Name(s) _____

Date: _____   Date when due: _____

Choice Option Menu Planning (CHOMP)

A menu of choices is something of a contract for individual students who want or need a way to record options in an independent study of choice. A menu can also be used with the whole class at the end of a unit of study as they choose ways to "show what they know."

Getting Ready

1. Start with the reproducible on page 168, or create your own menu of choices.
2. Make one copy of the menu for each child in the class.

The Process

1. Distribute the menus to the students.
2. Explain that each student is to choose four activities from the card (or three, with an additional choice proposed by the student) to show what he has learned.
3. Have students make their choices and complete their tasks.
4. Ask students to share their results with the class.

You can adapt the CHOMP menu to suit individual students and/or different areas of study.

Choice Option Menu

Student: *Christopher*   Topic: *Tomie dePaola*
Date: *11/1/04*   Date due: *11/15/04*

Choose four activities that you can complete to show the class what you've learned in your topic research. If you prefer, you may, with approval, choose three options from those below and then, for the fourth option, substitute something that isn't on the chart. Write one choice on each line.

1. *Picture Smart*
2. *Number Smart*
3. *People Smart*
4. *Compare and Contrast*

Alternative choice: _____   Teacher okay: _____

Word Smart	Compare and Contrast	Picture Smart
Read the *Secret Place* Poem. Write about your "secret place." What do you like to do when you go there?	Compare *The Art Lesson* with one of dePaola's other books. Look at characters, settings, problems, and solutions. Create a graphic organizer to show the similarities and differences you find.	Write a comparison of the illustrations in two books that dePaola illustrated. What do you notice about Tomie's illustrations? Are there any repeating themes? What are they? Draw a person or an animal as if you were Tomie.
Body Smart Choose a dePaola book as the basis for a Reader's Theater that you create. Be prepared to share it with the class. Ask classmates to help you.	**Think Smart** Many of Tomie's books involve grandparents. Draw a picture of you as you appear today. Draw another picture of how you will look when you're old enough to be a grandparent. Write how you will have changed.	**Number Smart** Create a graphic organizer to show how Tomie uses food and grandparents in his stories.
People Smart Survey the class to find out each person's favorite Tomie dePaola book. Create a visual to share your results.	**Self-Smart** Read at least four of Tomie's books. Prepare a five-minute presentation for the class as if you were doing a documentary on the themes and art of Tomie's books.	**Go Beyond Books** Interview a teacher, parent, or someone else who knows a lot about children's literature. Ask questions that would give you some facts and some opinions about Tomie. Tape the interview and play it for the class.

PURPOSE
To offer different kinds of learners alternatives to traditional written reports

INTELLIGENCES
Construction learner
Nature learner
Number learner
On-my-own learner
On-the-move learner
Rhythmic learner
With-friends learner
Word learner

LEARNING STYLES
Auditory learner
Tactile/kinesthetic learner
Visual learner

GROUP SIZE
Individual

SKILLS
Categorizing
Comparing/contrasting
Creative expression
Evaluating
Fix-up strategies
Following directions
Imaging
Inferring
Organization
Predicting/confirming
Problem-solving
Questioning
Sequencing
Synthesizing

AGE GROUP
Older

Choice Option Menu

Student: _____ Topic: _____

Date: _____ Date due: _____

Choose four activities that you can complete to show the class what you've learned in your topic research. If you prefer, you may, with approval, choose three options from those below and then, for the fourth option, substitute something that isn't on the chart. Write one choice on each line.

1. _____
2. _____
3. _____
4. _____

Alternative choice: _____ Teacher okay: _____

Word Smart	**Compare and Contrast**	**Picture Smart**
Prepare a lesson to teach to the class. Involve the other students. You may make up a game, conduct a panel discussion, or find another way to involve the class.	Create a visual way to look at two parts of your topic. Show how they are alike and how they are different.	Create a visual about your topic that you can present to the class. This can be computer-generated or your own art.
Body Smart	**Think Smart**	**Number Smart**
Make up a play, a Reader's Theater, a dramatic reading, or a pantomime. Or act something out as if you were playing "Charades," and let the class guess what you're showing.	How could your topic change in 20 years? Create a mock newscast or newspaper to share your ideas.	Use a graphic organizer to show the gist of your topic, or create a map that shows the setting of your report. Include a scale to indicate relative distances.
People Smart	**Self-Smart**	**Go Beyond Books**
Create a survey on your topic, and ask class members to answer the questions on your survey. Create a graphic to share the results.	Create an unusual way to share your knowledge. You may use music, rap, rhyme, or something similar that you choose.	Conduct and tape an interview with an "expert," and then play the interview for the class. Or search the Web for more information about the topic of your book. Add written personal comments on what you found out.

Rubrics and Posters for Your Classroom

RUBRICS Overview

A rubric is a set of guidelines for measuring progress toward a standard or objective. Having a rubric ensures that students and teachers share the same understanding of how progress will be measured and what constitutes mastery of that skill or goal. Unlike letter grades, rubrics allow you to measure a child's progress by identifying which skills she has mastered and which need work.

Rubrics can be developed by individual teachers, schools, or districts, but the most powerful rubrics are the ones that are developed in concert with the students. Children are very much aware of what constitutes each level of work in their classroom. With teacher guidance, they can help identify what a "good job" looks like in a particular project.

A rubric can be written as a checklist, as a numerical evaluation, or as a matrix with space for anecdotal examples. Just be sure that your students understand what they need to do or how they need to perform to attain each level. Students who are informed feel more secure and confident about their performance.

The following pages contain some sample rubrics for the language arts segment of your curriculum. Think of each of them as a jumping-off point for creating rubrics that are customized for your classroom.

Write Your Own Rubrics

Once you start using rubrics in your classroom, you'll want to create your own to cover other situations. Here are some guidelines to consider as you do that.

- Identify a skill to be worked on.
- Determine what this skill would look like at the different levels of development.
- Decide how can you observe and measure progress.
- Write out objectives that are achievable for students in the grade level you teach.
- State your objectives clearly.
- Word the description for each level of achievement so that students, parents, and other teachers share the same understanding of what is expected.
- Write all objectives in positive terms.

Reading Assessment Rubric

Student name _____

The goal of this rubric is to measure the growth of student reading skills over time. The rubric allows you to focus on one child at a time and to adjust instruction as necessary, based on your findings.

SCALE: 4—consistently
3—frequently
2—rarely/inconsistently
1—seldom/never

_____ Selects reading as an activity for free time

_____ Reads self-selected books at current grade level

_____ Reads a variety of literary genre (fiction, nonfiction, poetry, drama, newspapers, magazines)

_____ In shared discussions, demonstrates understanding of literature read in class

_____ Responds to literature in writing

_____ Demonstrates understanding of vocabulary terms by elaborating on word meanings and/or using the terms in other sentences

_____ Uses literary language (alliteration, similes, synthesis, and so on) in writing and speaking

_____ Demonstrates the use of different strategies (inferring, summarizing, predicting, and so on) through journaling and/or graphic organizers appropriate for grade level

_____ Adjusts reading strategies to fit genre

_____ Identifies parts of book (chapter, table of contents, glossary, and so on)

_____ Makes appropriate prediction of outcome of story

_____ Is able to retell story (characters and significant events in correct sequence)

_____ Is able to summarize the story's message in one or two sentences

_____ Recognizes differences between fact and opinion

_____ Recognizes differences between fact and fiction

_____ Uses appropriate reference materials (dictionary, atlas, thesaurus, Internet)

Writing Assessment Rubric

Student name _____

SCALE: 4—consistently
             3—frequently
             2—rarely/inconsistently
             1—seldom/never

_____ Views writing as a tool to give information and to gain it (by clarifying student's own thinking)

_____ Selects appropriate, relevant writing topics

_____ Writes daily

_____ Writes for a variety of purposes (letters, stories, journals, etc.)

_____ Writes for a given audience

_____ Demonstrates knowledge of the conventions of print (punctuation and capitalization)

_____ Demonstrates knowledge of the conventions of grammar and spelling

_____ Writes research reports using a variety of resources (reference books, first-hand sources, Internet, and so on)

_____ Writes in the content area on a regular basis

_____ Uses the writing process (draft, edit, rewrite, and so on)

_____ Adjusts writing to fit the genre or purpose

_____ Uses appropriate reference materials (dictionary, atlas, thesaurus, Internet)

_____ Writes poetry

_____ Writes drama

_____ Maintains a personal journal of collected wonderings, quotes, and ideas for future writing

_____ Uses literary language (similes, idioms, onomatopoeia) in writing

Listening Assessment Rubric

As you observe each student working on his Monthly Book Project or any other group sharing activity, you'll want to make specific notes about his behavior so that you can keep track of how he develops throughout the year. Consider these guidelines as you complete your assessments.

Once you've done this, share the results with students and parents, and then store progressive assessments in each student's folder so that you can refer to them for conferences and reporting.

1. Developing listener:
   a. often interrupts
   b. has a hard time paying attention to oral presentations
   c. loses thread of story or conversation
   d. often asks for things to be repeated
   e. has difficulty following directions

2. Capable listener:
   a. listens to others without interrupting
   b. usually is attentive to speaker and discussions
   c. follows oral directions

3. Strong listener:
   a. is interactive (listens, adds to, and amplifies other speakers' comments without taking over)
   b. listens to others
   c. maintains appropriate attention span
   d. focuses on speaker
   e. responds immediately to oral directions

ASSESSMENT:	DATE AND BEST EXAMPLE:	COMMENTS:
Developing listener	September—When John is asked to pack up his backpack and put his chair away, he can usually remember to do only one or the other.	I'll make sure that John is looking at me when I speak, and have him repeat both requests to me.
Capable listener	January—John is successfully completing two- and three-step directions, but I have to encourage him to focus and not dawdle.	Provide rewards for quick and immediate compliance —stickers, stamps, line leader.
Strong listener	April—John is consistently following directions promptly.	John is ready for first grade!

Speaking Assessment Rubric

1. Developing speaker:
   a. rarely contributes to class discussions
   b. has difficulty speaking in complete sentences
   c. may be reluctant to speak

2. Capable speaker:
   a. takes part in class discussions and stays on topic
   b. expresses ideas in complete sentences
   c. speaks loudly and clearly
   d. is able to speak to and build on others' ideas

3. Strong speaker:
   a. consistently makes relevant contributions to class discussions while staying on the topic
   b. expresses ideas with elaboration and support
   c. speaks loudly, clearly, and with expression
   d. is sure of self and needs no encouragement to enter conversation
   e. responds immediately to oral directions

ASSESSMENT:	DATE AND BEST EXAMPLE:	COMMENTS:
Developing speaker	September—Gives one or two responses to a question; needs to be prompted to give additional information.	Give him more wait-time; work one-on-one using pictures, retelling the story.
Capable speaker	January—Speaks in complete sentences, but doesn't go beyond one or two sentences.	Ask for more elaboration.
Strong speaker	April—Dominates the discussion, always contributing several points.	Encourage child to have dialogues and not monologues.

Observational Checklist for Reading Behaviors and Strategies

Beginning readers need to learn several ways to determine what a word means. Use the checklist below as you observe your students either in guided reading or during one-on-one reading. It's important that you make these kinds of observations on a regular basis, both to inform your teaching and to urge your students on to the next level of reading. Your goals are to track students' progress and to identify those skills that still need work. Remind yourself that every time your children leave your reading session, they should have learned something new about reading.

Child's name: _____ Date: _____

Directionality __ knows where to start on a page __ reads from left to right __ return sweeps __ reads top to bottom	**One-to-one correspondence** __ matches spoken to written word __ rereads to make word match
High-frequency words __ reads (number) of words from Dolch list __ is able to locate words on the word wall for spelling	**Unknown words** __ can locate unknown word using letters and sounds ("It's a picture of a dog. Can you find the word 'dog' in the sentence under the picture?")
Determining meaning __ uses pictures __ uses story __ uses background knowledge __ uses what makes sense __ rereads	**Structure** __ asks, "Does it sound right?" __ asks, "Does it sound like the way we say it in English?" __ rereads for how it sounds
Visual clues __ matches spoken word to printed word __ checks beginning, middle, and end __ uses sound and chunks to solve unknown words	**Monitoring** __ recognizes when makes an error (may be unsure of how to fix the error)
Cross-checking __ uses picture, meaning, structure, and visual clues __ rereads and uses more than one source to check information	**Self-correcting** __ recognizes when makes an error and is able to fix it

POSTERS FOR YOUR CLASSROOM
Overview

It's good to have posters in your classroom to remind students of what the rules are. It's even better if those posters list rules that the students had some part in creating. Start with the reproducibles on the following pages, and enlarge them onto large sheets of paper. Place the posters around the room. Then, working with one poster at a time, brainstorm with your class what the guidelines for behavior in class might be. Your role will be to guide the process so that classroom rules are stated in a positive manner. Make sure that the posters say what *should* be happening in the class, rather than what isn't allowed. Creating the posters with the class is an opportunity for all of you to start to define your classroom community. After the initial brainstorming session is over, encourage the students to continue to add to the posters or refine them to fit your particular classroom needs.

Explain to your students that these rules are in place during

- Lunch
- Recess
- Hallway/Transition times
- Paired-work time
- Small-group interactions
- Literacy circles
- Book clubs
- Field trips
- And any other time when there is any student interaction!

Following the four posters on classroom management is a second set of posters. These are posters listing instructions for centers. They can be used with any piece of literature your students are currently reading. Invite students to work individually or in pairs to complete the activities described on each poster. When they've finished, post the resulting graphic organizers or literary responses in the center or around the room—or share them with the whole class at the end of the literacy block.

You can use these posters in many ways. For example:

- Copy a poster onto card stock, laminate it, and display it in the Literacy Center.
- Enlarge it to poster size.
- Rewrite it onto chart paper.
- If the poster refers to a graphic organizer, place several copies of an appropriate graphic organizer in a special location, and let students take them back to their desks to complete the organizers.

Being ACCOUNTABLE means:

* being respectful
* showing self-control
* being responsible
* having self-discipline

In ACCOUNTABLE talk, we:

* make eye contact with each other

* wait until others are finished speaking before we begin

* speak to the entire group

* lean in and turn our heads to hear

* make sure we clear up confusion by questioning or talking more

Ways To Say More When You
AGREE

I understand and would like to add . . .

That really makes sense because . . .

That's really smart because . . .

What To Say When You
DISAGREE

I don't think that's true
because . . .

I know that's
your opinion but . . .

Character Analysis

Read the story.

Complete a graphic organizer by:

☀ identifying the main character

☀ listing four things you noticed about that character

☀ telling where in the text you found each characteristic you listed

Listening Post

Listen to the book
while you read along.

Write in your response log:

✳ the main idea

✳ your feelings about one of
the characters

✳ what you think will happen
next and why

✳ how you would change the story
to make it more interesting

Share one of
your responses
with someone in
your group.

How to Make Something

→ Read the instructions.

→ Make one for yourself.

→ Write in your response log:
  ✔ what you did
  ✔ what materials you used
  ✔ in what order you did each step

→ Leave what you made on the bulletin board.

Did You Know ...?
READING NONFICTION

★ Read the text two times.

★ Write down four facts that you found that were new to you.

★ Write your facts in a web organizer.

★ Compare your organizer to someone else's.

★ Discuss how they are alike and/or different.

★ Decide what else was in the text that is missing from your "fact" finds. Add those things to the web.

Resources

Internet Connections for Teachers

These sites contain downloads for teacher tools, lesson plans, and sample texts. Check them out!

www.aaronshep.com
(downloadable Reader's Theater; different reading levels)

www.eduscapes.com
(integrates technology and education; emphasizes thematic topics)

www.lessonplanspage.com
(more than 2,000 lesson plans designed for classes from PreK through12th grade)

www.lindahoyt.com
(free lessons, tools, newsletters)

www.nwrel.org
(programs and projects/assessments; excellent source of lesson plans for all grade levels in reading and writing)

www.readingatoz.com
(requires a subscription; has downloadable leveled texts and lesson plans)

www.readinglady.com
(several downloads for classroom charts and work sheets)

www.readwritethink.org
(contains lesson plans and many links to other related sites)

www.U46teachers.org /mosaic/tools/tools.htm
(source of lesson plans and downloadable materials based on the book *Mosaic of Thought: Teaching Comprehension in a Reader's Workshop* by Ellin O. Keene & Susan Zimmermann)

www.50states.com
(source of blank maps, trivia, and facts about each of the 50 states; several links to related sites)

www.puzzlemaker.com
(create your own crossword puzzles, search-a-words, mazes, etc.)

SEARCH ENGINES:

www.askjeeves.com
www.google.com
www.yahooligans.com

Print Resources

Allen, Janet. *On the Same Page: Shared Reading Beyond the Primary Grades.* Portland, ME: Stenhouse Publishers, 2002.

Allington, Richard L. *What Really Matters for Struggling Readers: Designing Research-Based Programs.* New York: Longman, 2001.

Armstrong, Thomas. *The Multiple Intelligences of Reading and Writing: Making the Words Come Alive.* Alexandria, VA: ASCD, 2003.

Buehl, Doug. *Classroom Strategies for Interactive Learning.* Newark, DE: International Reading Association, 2001.

Calkins, Lucy C. *The Art of Teaching Reading.* New York: Longman, 2001.

Chapman, Carolyn, and Rita King. *Differentiated Instructional Strategies for Reading in the Content Areas.* Thousand Oaks, CA: Corwin Press, 2003.

Duke, Nell K., and P. David Pearson. "Effective Practices for Developing Reading Comprehension," in *What Research Has to Say About Reading Instruction.* Newark, DE: International Reading Association, 2002.

Gardner, Howard. *Multiple Intelligences: The Theory in Practice.* New York: Basic Books, 1993.

Harvey, Stephanie. *Nonfiction Matters: Reading, Writing, and Research in Grades 3–8.* Portland, ME: Stenhouse Publishers, 1998.

Hindley, Joanne. *In the Company of Children.* Portland, ME: Stenhouse Publishers, 1996.

Hoyt, Linda. "Many Ways of Knowing: Using drama, oral interactions, and the visual arts to enhance reading comprehension." *The Reading Teacher,* 45 (8, 1992): 580–84.

Hoyt, Linda. *Revisit, Reflect, Retell.* Portsmouth, NH: Heinemann, 1999.

Jensen, Eric. *Arts with the Brain in Mind.* Alexandria, VA: ASCD, 2001.

_____. *Teaching with the Brain in Mind.* Alexandria, VA: ASCD, 1998.

Keene, Ellin O., and Susan Zimmermann. *Mosaic of Thought: Teaching Comprehension in a Reader's Workshop.* Portsmouth, NH: Heinemann, 1997.

Miller, Debbie. *Reading with Meaning: Teaching Comprehension in the Primary Grades.* Portland, ME: Stenhouse Publishers, 2002.

Opitz, Michael F., and Michael P. Ford. *Reaching Readers: Flexible and Innovative Strategies for Guided Reading.* Portsmouth, NH: Heinemann, 2001.

Routman, Regie. *Reading Essentials: The Specifics You Need to Teach Reading Well.* Portsmouth, NH: Heinemann, 2002.

Szymusiak, Karen, and Franki Sibberson. *Beyond Leveled Books: Supporting Transitional Readers in Grades 2–5.* Portland, ME: Stenhouse Publishers, 2001.

Tomlinson, Carol A. *The Differentiated Classroom: Responding to the Needs of All Learners.* Alexandria, VA: ASCD, 1999.

Index

Note: Page numbers in *italics* refer to reproducibles.

Note: Page numbers in *italics* refer to reproducibles.

Note: Page numbers in *italics* refer to reproducibles.

Note: Page numbers in *italics* refer to reproducibles.

Note: Page numbers in *italics* refer to reproducibles.